DREAMING BIGGER

Jewish Leadership for Teens

Dr. Erica Brown and Rabbi Dr. Benji Levy

BEHRMAN HOUSE

www.behrmanhouse.com

In Memory of
Rabbi Lord Jonathan Sacks
(1948–2020)
Mentor
Light
Leader

Published by Behrman House, Inc.
Millburn, New Jersey 07041
www.behrmanhouse.com

ISBN 978-1-68115-095-6

Published with support from the Mayberg Center for Jewish Education and Leadership at The George Washington University and KeshevCenter.com based in Jerusalem Israel.

Poem by Sophia Zalik used with permission of Helen Zalik.

Library of Congress Control Number: 2022936217

Illustrations by Gal Weisman and Shlomo Blass
Design by Tim Holtz
Cover design by Penina Shtauber and Tim Holtz
Edited by Dena Neusner and Tzivia MacLeod

Printed in the United States of America

9 8 7 6 5 4 3 2 1

Contents

PART I   Leading Yourself

"If I Am Not for Myself, Who Will Be for Me?"

INTRODUCTION
Dreaming Bigger

Dear Teen Leader,

Teens are changing the world. You are changing *our* world.

Teen leaders are planning, protesting, and raising the social consciousness of those around them. They are questioning the status quo, using technology to do good, and pushing others to do so as well. Teens are leading others. In sports, through extramural activities, and in clubs.

They're helping kids with cancer and teaching residents of senior facilities how to use the internet. They're holding bake sales and car washes for tzedakah and working as counselors in day camps and overnight camps, youth movements, and travel programs. Does this sound like you? For example . . .

- Do you look at problems others ignore? ✔
- Do you have a strong desire to fix what's broken? ✓
- Do you find joy in helping others? ✔
- Do you want to do something big in the world? ✔

If you're reading this book, chances are the answer is yes to at least one of these questions. Maybe you want to help neighbors or those in need through community service, advocate for a political cause, or run a debate club. You want to create change locally or globally—or both.

We know more about Jewish teens today than we've ever known before. Drs. Arielle Levites and Liat Sayfan surveyed over fifteen thousand teens in their groundbreaking study "Gen Z Now: Understanding and Connecting with Today's Jewish Teens." Their findings tell us a lot about how Jewish teens feel about Judaism and their role in it. Teens today have a strong sense of self and feel proud to be Jewish. They enjoy learning about other Jewish communities and Jewish holidays and feel positive about celebrating them. They value strong friendships, family bonds, and the opportunity to be mentored. They want to be part of the Jewish people and have a positive relationship with the people and State of Israel. They seek language to express their spiritual journeys and their struggles. They also want to make a difference in the communities in which they live and the world at large.

Today's Jewish teens are a generation of doers and creative thinkers who have the skills and confidence to know they don't have to ask permission or wait for adults to make the world a kinder, better place.

What the research tells us are things you may already know because you are now designing your Jewish future. Now's the time to find your voice and your causes, to think about your influence, mission, and purpose, and to bring others along with you to do good in the world. You are leading. You are dreaming bigger.

Judaism is a continuous story of dreams and dreamers. In the Torah, Jacob, as a teenager, "had a dream; a ladder was set on the ground and its top reached to the sky, and angels of God were going up and down on it." (Genesis 28:12) It was a sacred dream about the connection between heaven and earth and his unique place between them. When he woke up, he knew that he had to have a family of his own and become a blessing to the world. Jacob nurtured that dream, held tightly to the promise of being a blessing to others, and made it his life's purpose.

The image of a ladder reaching to heaven suggests the climb each of us can make to meet our goals and aspirations. The higher we go, the more we can look down at where we've come from and look up to where we still want to go. The image of a ladder is helpful in another way: while striving heavenward, acting on their dreams, leaders must keep their feet planted firmly on the ground.

● What do you usually dream about?

● Describe a dream that had an influence on your life.

Great leadership is built on big dreams. Shimon Peres, the ninth president of the State of Israel, who gave decades to public service, once offered this leadership advice:

> People sometimes ask me: if you look back, what were your
> biggest mistakes? I will answer: we thought we had great dreams.
> And now we understand that they were not so great. Dream big.
> The bigger your dream, the more you will achieve.

Peres was not the only leader to believe in the power of dreams. Rabbi Lord Jonathan Sacks, who was the chief rabbi of the United Hebrew Congregations of the Commonwealth and a great Jewish leader, once wrote, "Dream dreams. Never be afraid to let your imagination soar."

Pay attention to your dreams. Nurture them and grow them. Act on them and be bold.

What are your big, audacious dreams?

Let's discover them.

Erica and Benji

How to Use This Book

The Talmudic sage Hillel first posed these three questions in a collection of Jewish wisdom called Pirkei Avot (Ethics of the Fathers). Each question is important on its own. But together, they remind us that in life and in leadership, we must begin with ourselves—our mission, our sense of purpose, and our unique skills and talents. Then we move beyond ourselves to see how we can make a meaningful contribution in the lives of others. While we may never finish the work, we can't wait another minute to begin making a difference. "If not now, when?"

> If I am not for myself, who will be for me? If I am only for myself, what am I? If not now, when?

In line with Hillel's saying, we've organized this book into three parts:

- Part I: Leading Yourself—"If I Am Not for Myself, Who Will Be for Me?" Understanding ourselves and how we lead.

- Part II: Leading Others—"If I Am Only for Myself, What Am I?" Our responsibility to others and how to lead effectively.

- Part III: Leading in Community—"If Not Now, When?" Leading to improve the world, starting today with issues that require teen leadership.

When you pick up this book, we encourage you to read it through to get a sense of where it may help you with your leadership or skip straight to what is most helpful to you right now. Need to raise some money? There's a chapter on fundraising. Need to give a speech and you're feeling nervous? Find some helpful guidelines in the chapter on communication. Struggling with issues of inclusion and trying to persuade others to join you? Take a look at the chapter on inclusion and diversity.

Throughout the book, you'll find "Inner Workouts" to help you reflect on your leadership, along with case studies that you can use alone or in groups. There's also lots of advice from leadership experts and other teens. Finally, most chapters end with a "Jewish Bright Spot" to share insights from Jewish texts and invite you to interpret them.

We hope the questions and exercises included in many of the chapters will ease you out of your comfort zone and toward new discoveries, because we all grow through challenging where we are now, taking risks, and stretching ourselves.

Before we wrote this book, we surveyed and spoke with over a hundred teen leaders from Australia, Canada, Israel, New Zealand, South Africa, the United Kingdom, and the United States. They told us how they were bringing their personalities, skills, thoughts, concerns, spirituality, religious observance, politics, sexual orientation, race, color, disabilities, and abilities to lead in the Jewish community and in the world.

Through these conversations, we discovered how teens think about their leadership, what excites them, and what pressures they're under. We learned how demanding it is to balance the time devoted to friends, homework, and volunteering, along with the challenge of building a résumé for college. We heard about peer pressure and other anxieties and how much teens want to experience more joy and confidence as they lead. We share parts of those conversations throughout this book. In some cases, we changed names or identifying details when teens preferred to remain anonymous. We're so grateful to everyone we spoke with for trusting us with their thoughts and ideas!

We also interviewed many professionals who work with teen leaders. We want to give a special shout-out to all the executive directors, CEOs, therapists, rabbis, nonprofit leaders, youth movement leaders, teachers, head counselors, and others who took the time to share their insights with us.

All the wisdom we gathered from other teen and adult leaders is just the beginning. Now it's your turn to make this leadership journey your own.

This book is part of a much bigger initiative that we invite you to give to, gain from, and be part of. We have created animations and masterclasses, an educator's guide and conversation cards, discussion forums and so much more, all of which can be found at DreamingBigger.org. We invite you to share your leadership insights with us and our growing teen leadership community.

Thanks for joining us. We're so glad you're here!

LEADING YOURSELF

If I am not for myself, who will be for me?

אִם אֵין אֲנִי לִי, מִי לִי?

Im ain ani li, mi li?

(PIRKEI AVOT 1:14)

1

DEFINING JEWISH LEADERSHIP

Before we jump into talking about Jewish leadership, let's define what leadership actually is: the act of moving a group of people or an organization to achieve a common goal. In the Jewish tradition, spiritual leadership is not about power. It's about serving others and influencing people to make positive change. It's about taking action that is inspired by values as part of a life driven by meaning. It's about having an inspiring role in the ongoing Jewish conversation.

Peter Drucker (1909–2005), a leadership expert, defined leadership as the lifting of human vision to "higher sights." This also means raising human "performance to a higher standard." It involves pushing people beyond what they thought of as their limits. John Quincy Adams (1767–1848), the sixth president of the United States, is attributed with saying, "If your actions inspire others to dream more, learn more, do more, and become more, you are a leader." Drucker and Adams saw their primary work as moving and growing others.

In Jewish leadership, helping others often stems from Jewish values such as tzedakah (charity as justice), *chesed* (loving-kindness), and *tikun olam* (healing the world). Thousands of Jewish heroes throughout history and in the present offer us leadership lessons and personal examples. Jewish leadership is enriched by Jewish learning.

According to Mark Charendoff, the president of the Maimonides Fund, a foundation dedicated to education and Jewish identity, "The Jews have a unique contribution to make . . . the Jewish community can help society be kinder, more generous, spiritual and closer to God—that may be the best and only way to transform society." Charendoff believes that Jewish texts and values are a pathway to help leaders raise the bar with "the highest level of ethics and meaning."

Dreaming Bigger

Liron Lipinsky Salitrik, who worked in Jewish education before joining the B'nai B'rith Youth Organization (BBYO), invites us to merge our Judaism with our leadership:

> To me, being Jewish and being a leader is the same. It's not like one day you're doing Jewish leadership and another you're leading. . . . You're not just Jewish on certain days of the week or in Jewish buildings with four walls. You carry Judaism with you everywhere.

Jewish leadership is about rising to the challenges of service and having an active and inspiring role in our evolving Jewish story. As the Torah unfolds, we meet many leaders who shaped the ancient Jewish world and beyond through their vision, sense of responsibility, and commitment: Isaac, Jacob, Rebecca, Joseph, Miriam, Moses, Samuel, David, Jeremiah, and Esther, to name but a few. They were all young people who matured into leadership, rising to meet a challenge and taking charge of a situation—often a crisis—and influencing others along the way. They had to make personal sacrifices, and they had plenty of "dragons" to slay on their way to becoming everyday heroes.

Inner Workout

- Name one of your personal heroes. Explain some of the ways in which they have influenced you or others.

- If you could wave a magic wand and make a real difference to any cause in the world, what would it be and why?

- What "dragon" would you have to slay to make this happen?

Let's meet some outstanding teen leaders—people who were inspired to become leaders and change our world for the better for many different reasons. First, two leaders you might already know who started as teens. Malala Yousafzai, a Pakistani activist for girls' education, is the world's youngest Nobel Prize laureate. When she was eleven, she started a blog for the BBC to document the hardships girls faced under the Taliban regime. At sixteen, she cowrote the international bestseller *I Am Malala*. Then there's Greta Thunberg, a Swedish environmental activist who began by convincing her parents to reduce their carbon footprint and then, at age fifteen, called a "school strike" for climate change outside the Swedish parliament, eventually leading twenty thousand students to join her in protests worldwide. The same year, she addressed the United Nations Climate Change Conference, and in 2019, she was included in Forbes 100 Most Powerful Women and named as *Time* magazine's Person of the Year.

There are also teens who are not household names (yet) who are using their voices for good. Asean Johnson was only nine when he made an impassioned speech opposing the Chicago mayor's proposal to close his school and forty-nine others in predominantly Black and Latino neighborhoods. "You should be investing in these schools, not closing them!" he said. His elementary school stayed open. When Asean was twelve, he spoke in Washington, DC, at a rally for hundreds of educators and activists supporting public education and social justice. Speaking through tears, he shared the tragedies he was witnessing: "I don't even know if I can make it past the age that I am with everything that's happening."

Rishab Jain is an inventor, researcher, developer, and YouTuber from Oregon. When he was thirteen, 3M named him one of America's top young scientists for developing a software tool that uses artificial intelligence to help doctors more accurately treat pancreatic cancer.

Melati and Isabel Wijsen are sisters and climate activists from Indonesia. At ages twelve and ten, they launched the "Bye Bye Plastic Bags" campaign to reduce harm to ocean life. They organized a cleanup that inspired twenty thousand people to join them in collecting sixty-five tons of plastic waste.

We also want to introduce you to some Jewish teen leaders who are changing the world as we know it.

Jamie Margolin is a former gymnast from Seattle. When she was fifteen, she cofounded the youth climate action organization Zero Hour, which aims to center the voices of teens in the conversation around climate and environmental justice through youth-led marches and protests. Jamie says:

> I felt a drive and passion to protect what was left for my future and my life. I was in second grade when I recognized this, but I didn't know how to take action until I was fourteen. No one tells kids how to take action.

Jamie says her Jewish background inspired her to get involved: "What I've learned from my Jewish values is that silence is complicity. We can't ignore things; we have to stand up for what we believe in."

When Arielle Geismar was seventeen, she won a Diller Tikkun Olam Award for creating NYC Says Enough, an organization that educates people about gun violence and promotes teen activism, connecting with more than twenty-three thousand people across partisan lines to create reform. She sees being a leader as a response to what she calls the "lockdown generation" created by the perilous intersection of gun violence, antisemitism, and white supremacy. Reflecting on two synagogue shooting incidents—at Chabad of Poway in California in 2019, and at the Tree of Life Congregation in Pennsylvania in 2018—Arielle said,

> The hatred of antisemitism and white supremacy is deeply woven into those incidents. Part of it is seeing my community being hurt by hatred. It's painful and traumatizing to many Jewish people who understand where this leads.

Like the other teen leaders we've met in this chapter, Arielle saw darkness in the world and brought her light to it, just as the biblical prophet Isaiah asked: "To open blind eyes; to remove a prisoner from confinement, dwellers in darkness from a dungeon." (Isaiah 42:7)

Our job every day is to see the darkness that others are in and share our light. We cannot slay every dragon, but we can slay some.

Jewish Bright Spot

The prophet Isaiah had a defining moment early in his mission when he saw that there was no one leading the Jewish people. God was looking for a leader and asked, "Whom shall I send? Who will go for us?" Isaiah's response: *Hineni*, which means "Here I am; send me." (Isaiah 6:8)

1. What do you think Isaiah meant when he said "Here I am"?

2. Why did he even need to say it?

3. Describe a "Here I am; send me" moment you've experienced.

2

WHO AM I?

When you lead, you often make discoveries about your identity, as well as your strengths and weaknesses. You think about your past, your present, your character, and the people who have influenced you. You think about what makes you different and what makes you unique.

Inner Workout

Time a minute on the clock and write one word (and only one) that describes YOU next to each of these roles (try to avoid clichés)—for example, *loyal* next to *friend*.

- Friend:

- Student:

- Leader:

- Jew:

- Volunteer:

- Sibling (if relevant):

On a scale of 1 to 10, with 1 being easy and 10 being hard, how difficult was it for you to come up with all seven words?

Which word was easiest to come up with? Why?

Which one was hardest? Why?

Now it's time to consider the skills you bring to your leadership. What is it that makes you shine?

Inner Workout

Make a list of your top five strengths:

1. _____

2. _____

3. _____

4. _____

5. _____

List five activities where your unique talents are on full display:

1. _____

2. _____

3. _____

4. _____

5. _____

Tom Rath, who writes and speaks on leadership in the workplace, says leaders need to focus on what they're good at: "A revision to the 'You-can-be-anything-you-want-to-be' maxim might be more accurate: You *cannot* be anything you want to be—but you *can* be a lot more of who you already are."

So instead of spending your life trying to be good at everything, Rath believes, you need to figure out who you are and then build on your talents instead of highlighting your weaknesses. "If you spend your life trying to be good at everything," he writes, "you will never be great at anything." Or as a Talmudic expression goes, "If you try to grab too much, you don't end up grabbing anything."

Lots of people, however, have FOMO (fear of missing out). They don't want to close any doors, so they sign up for everything: teams, committees, and clubs. Then they sometimes find they're not doing a good job at anything. Are you feeling like you've spread yourself too thin?

Leading well involves figuring out what we can change and what we cannot. That work starts with ourselves.

Jewish Bright Spot

Rabbi Moshe Chaim Luzzatto (1707–1746) was an Italian scholar who wrote one of the most widely studied Jewish books of self-improvement, *The Path of the Just*. There he discusses purity, humility, saintliness, and how to manage anger, envy, and desire. He felt it was critically important to take stock of oneself and be honest with shortcomings: "A person must constantly—at all times, and particularly during a regularly appointed time of solitude—reflect upon the true path that a person must walk upon. After engaging in such reflection, one must come to consider whether or not one's deeds travel along this path."

1. What do you think Rabbi Luzzatto means by one's deeds traveling along a path?

2. Do you set aside regular times to reflect on your leadership and think about your own path? If not, how might you do that?

3. Think of something you tried to change when what you really needed to change was yourself.

3

SAYING NO AND SAYING YES

Great leadership involves saying yes. With the word *yes* we open ourselves up to new possibilities. Every yes is also a risk; we can never know completely what we are agreeing to. In the Torah, extraordinary leaders such as Isaiah (as we mentioned in chapter 1), along with Abraham, Moses, and others, used the word *hineni*—"I am fully and totally present and committed as I accept this responsibility"—as their yes. They understood that *hineni* meant accepting all the duties, obligations, and uncertainty of leadership. We all want to say those empowering three letters: *Y-E-S*. As leaders, we don't want to disappoint others. We want to serve them, and we should. Plus, it feels great to say yes; it opens worlds and opens us up to new possibilities.

But part of the self-awareness we talked about in the previous chapter involves knowing when to say no as a leader. Saying yes to everything can deplete us. We might even resent giving time and effort to something that doesn't nourish us or feel worthwhile. When we do that, we run out of energy to do what we really care about and be with people we really want to spend time with.

Inner Workout

- Name a "yes" you said that you later regretted.

- Describe the regret you experienced and why you felt that way.

- Why did you say yes in the first place?

Chana Kaplan, who runs a Washington, DC–area branch of Friendship Circle, a Jewish nonprofit that pairs teen volunteers with other teens who have mental and physical challenges, has seen what happens close up when volunteers over-commit. "I tell them if you can't commit, don't do it at all," Kaplan explains. That may sound harsh, but Kaplan has also seen the heartbreak of a kid with cancer or Down syndrome who is expecting a visitor when that visitor never shows up.

It's better *not* to take on a responsibility than to say yes and not see it through. We feel guilty saying no; it never feels good, especially if friends or teachers are the ones who are asking. But *no* may be the most important word in your leadership. It helps you prioritize and determine what *you* really care about.

A Better, Kinder Yes

Before you say yes to another leadership task or responsibility, ask yourself these seven questions. You might want to talk through your answers with someone or write them down.

1. Do I want to say yes? What will I gain from saying yes?

2. When I say yes to this, what or who am I saying no to?

3. How do I say no in the kindest way possible?

4. Can I renegotiate the request with different terms or timing?

5. Can anyone else do this job or role?

6. Is now the right time for me?

7. Will I resent the task I am saying yes to later?

Sometimes we want to say no but we can't find the right words. If that happens, try softening the message by starting on a positive note—for example, "I'd love to, but this year I'm committed to getting my college applications done early," or "I really appreciate that you thought of me, but this really isn't my passion or area of expertise." In short, as a wise friend once said, if a person has the chutzpah to ask, you can have the chutzpah to say no. Saying no can be hard, but it gets a lot easier with practice. Each no helps us say a bigger yes to the things we truly care about.

Make sure that when you *do* say yes, you mean it. The Talmud states that when we say yes, it should be a firm yes; and when we say no, it should be a firm no. We should be sure of what we want to do. While some people say yes too often, some don't say it often enough. Firmly saying yes and no helps us step up to opportunities for growth and contribution.

Jewish Bright Spot

At Mount Sinai, the Israelites said yes together to the Ten Commandments, even though they did not understand fully how this yes would change their future: "All the people answered as one, saying, 'All that Adonai has spoken we will do!'" (Exodus 19:8) The ancient Israelites were committed to listening and to doing.

1. Why was this yes important?

2. What is the power of saying yes together as a group? What is the danger?

3. Describe a yes you said even though you didn't understand everything that was involved.

Why Me?
Quieting Your Inner Critic

So you're going to a big school event. You're wearing a great new shirt, and your hair looks perfect. You're excited, especially since you want to impress someone there. You have a quick look in the mirror before you leave. Uh-oh. You spot a pimple. Suddenly all you want to do is stay home, get under your covers, and sleep until it goes away.

We seem hardwired to always find one little fault and blow it up so it's all we see. Not just physical faults, like pimples, but on bad days, the way we look at ourselves. When asked about our strengths and weaknesses, so often we can go on and on about what we're doing badly and shortchange ourselves about what we're doing right. We intentionally started this conversation about leadership with your strengths, to counter this habit. But we also need to explore the ways you wish you were stronger or better.

Rachel, for example, was a youth leader in her synagogue, the editor of her high school yearbook, and a camp counselor. She's always been tough on herself, and she talked to us about the anxiety she felt when trying to earn the respect of the people she was leading: "I had a fear of making a mistake and letting people down." As a result, Rachel didn't trust her instincts. When we have our own or other people's negative voices in our heads, we can't hear ourselves or recognize what we're doing right.

Something similar happened to Jeremy, who is involved in Young Judea and has also been a camp counselor for many years. He once ran a camping trip that became what he calls a "mild mess." Campers weren't listening. His programs weren't working. He thought he was a total failure. He blamed himself. Eventually he worked through the situation rationally and slowly: "I just kept pushing forward and took it one step at a time."

Rachel and Jeremy are experiencing what has been termed "impostor syndrome," a deep feeling of inadequacy that persists despite a person's evident success. If you suffer from imposter syndrome (and we all do at times), you might be weighed down by chronic self-doubt. It can be hard to quiet that inner critic.

You may worry that any minute someone else is going to call you out as a fraud. A voice in your head says, "I have no idea what I'm doing and soon everyone else will realize it, too."

Maybe you don't have a big dream yet and the idea of doing anything heroic sounds far-fetched. Maybe you've lost sight of your talents. Everyone tells you to be yourself. That would be fantastic advice—if you knew who you were!

You may believe that the word *leader* implies that you've figured it all out. You're a role model. You know yourself. Right?

Wrong. Leaders don't know everything. They're always learning on the job.

Inner Workout

What are three things your inner critic shouts?

1.

2.

3.

Here's a little secret—even the most successful leaders feel inadequate sometimes. Acknowledge the moments when you're feeling inadequate. People will respect you more for being yourself and recognizing your doubts.

In the Torah, God tells Moses to take the Jews from slavery to freedom. To do so, Moses would have to challenge Pharaoh, the king of Egypt. Instead of an enthusiastic yes, Moses responds with a question: "Who am I?" (Exodus 3:11)

In a sense, Moses was saying, "I am not worthy of leading. I can't do this. I don't know how. Why did you pick me?"

You've probably had your own Moses moment. Maybe you weren't sure you were up to the responsibility you'd been given. Maybe you looked in the mirror and thought, "I don't have the self-confidence, skills, or background for this. Pick someone else."

We can all be so tough on ourselves that we miss our sparkle, competency, and potential. God saw something in Moses that Moses could not see in himself. Chances are that if you're reading this book, someone else sees that in you, too.

Jewish Bright Spot

Moses said many times that he couldn't accept the leadership assignment God had given him: to free the Jews from Egyptian slavery. He didn't think anyone would believe in him. He also famously said these words: "Please, O Adonai, I have never been a man of words, either in times past or now that You have spoken to Your servant; I am slow of speech and slow of tongue." (Exodus 4:10)

1. What was Moses's inner critic shouting?

2. What was holding Moses back and what helped him accept his leadership role anyway?

3. Describe one of your Moses moments.

GROWING AND CHANGING AS A LEADER

Learning to quiet your inner critic is crucial to seeing yourself as a leader, but that doesn't mean you stop working on yourself. We're all constantly evolving. We set goals and commit to change. We fail. We try again. We try to become better versions of ourselves: more honest, kinder, more ambitious, and more generous. It's like standing on tiptoe to reach something high up that you can see but can't yet touch.

Inner Workout

Stand up tall and reach your hands up to their highest point. Now reach them a bit higher. You see? You can always reach a little bit higher than you originally thought.

Part of the process of self-improvement is recognizing that we're all a work in progress. Business professor and leadership expert Warren Bennis used to say that "no one can teach you how to become yourself . . . except you." He encourages leaders to accept four basic principles about themselves:

1. You are your own best teacher.

2. Accept responsibility. Blame no one.

3. You can learn anything you want to learn.

4. True understanding comes from reflecting on your experience.

Learning to lead is a lot like learning to drive. You control the direction of the car and where it's going. You first learn to drive slowly and carefully. You try to improve until you can drive with ease. Mistakes you make behind the wheel are yours alone. You can learn to be a better driver by analyzing your mistakes and working on them.

Because leaders are responsible for others, their mistakes sometimes have a broader impact and can even cause pain. Although we have the opportunity to be better every single day, Jews have one day a year—Yom Kippur, the holiest day on the Jewish calendar—to confess our wrongs on the road to self-improvement; to put ourselves, as drivers, on a better road forward.

Inner Workout

On Yom Kippur, we recite Viduy, a private list of confessions in which we mention many of the areas where we could have done better in the past year, such as having more respect for teachers and parents or not speaking badly about others. Let's adapt the confessional formula of Viduy to identify some leadership mistakes that could use improvement:

● For the leadership mistake of . . .

● For the leadership mistake of . . .

● For the leadership mistake of . . .

Many teen leaders we spoke to said they aren't great at delegating to others because they're trying too hard to do everything themselves. That's a great example of a "leadership mistake," as we heard from Brooke, a sixteen-year-old who was in the American Jewish Committee Leaders for Tomorrow doing Israel advocacy and fighting antisemitism and has been a leader in her synagogue's Washington, DC–area youth movement:

When I'm working with a group, I tend to want to do it all myself. It's challenging to hold myself back and make sure people participate equally. I've worked on myself, and I'm in a very good place with that. When I was younger, I felt that to do something right meant to do it my way. It got to a point where I was under so much stress that I couldn't do it all myself.

Brooke realized that she had to work within her own limitations. When she acknowledged the challenge, started holding back, and made sure others had a chance to participate, she discovered that she was a more effective leader.

Knowing yourself is a superpower.

Improving yourself is a gift.

Jewish Bright Spot

Maimonides (circa 1138–1204) was a great scholar and physician. He begins "The Laws of Repentance," a part of his *Mishneh Torah*, with a seemingly simple question: "What is repentance?" His answer could take a whole lifetime to unpack: "The sinner shall cease sinning, and remove sin from his thoughts, and wholeheartedly conclude not to do it again . . . he will also experience regret."

1. Most people who lead do so with the best of intentions. But sometimes we fall short of this goal. Sometimes it's not enough to stop what you're doing wrong. According to Maimonides, you must get rid of the desire itself. Can you think of a time when you were able to do that?

2. What role does regret play in stimulating change?

3. Think of a leadership regret you have. While you may not be able to change things that happened in the past, what can you do about it now, in the present?

6
LEADING AND ROLE MODELING

Adam is from London and has served in leadership roles at school and in youth movements in England, Australia, Israel, and the US, yet even he feels inadequate sometimes. "I don't feel qualified to be a role model," he says. "I mean, who am I to be an example to others? I didn't do anything special; I just got here by luck."

From talking with Adam, we know that's not true; few teens are as qualified as Adam is. The fact that, over and over again, he's seen a need and worked hard to fill it isn't just luck. But like many teen leaders, Adam can't see it for himself. That's because he's still figuring himself out *while* he's leading and *when* he's leading. That means he's going to make mistakes, and that's how he's going to learn.

The moment you step into a leadership role, other people start looking up to you and judging you. They see you differently—even if you don't feel different. They observe and may even comment on the decisions you make, the way you present yourself, and the way you treat others. They watch how you talk to adults, how you interact with friends. They pay attention to your body language, the way you dress, the way you act, and whether you follow rules or break them. They notice if you gossip or put down others who disagree with you. Leadership may be a privilege, but being watched can feel like a burden. It can also help you rise to your best self. It's important for Adam to let others know that he's learning, kind of like the sign that new drivers put on their cars that reads "Student Driver. Please Be Patient."

Student driver
please be patient

Think of a person who you consider a role model. In one minute, put down all the nouns, verbs, and adjectives you associate with that person.

● Nouns:

● Verbs:

● Adjectives:

Now make a word cloud of those words, writing each word bigger or smaller according to how important that quality is to you.

Being a role model doesn't just mean who you are when you're in public spaces or in front of a crowd. As a teen leader, you represent whatever it is you lead—your group, team, club, or organization—even when you're not in that setting. Leaders are often measured by their consistency and whether they are living up to their promises and values.

When you inspire people, they will try to imitate you, and that's where we see the importance of recognizing yourself as a role model. We met Jeremy in an earlier chapter. When he was working with younger campers, he started to recognize his influence on their behavior: "I try to lead by example. If I do something and people start to follow, that means I have accomplished something." Jeremy takes this responsibility seriously, in part from observing his own Jewish role models and their deep feelings of responsibility for the welfare of others. "Judaism is a part of who I am, so it leaks into everything I do," Jeremy says.

Josh is excited to begin his first summer as a camp counselor. One week into the summer, he notices that all the fourth graders in his bunk are casually using curse words in conversation. Josh reprimands the kids for speaking this way. The week goes on and nothing changes, despite Josh's constant comments to his bunk. He brings it up in a staff meeting one evening. All the counselors agree that they will encourage their bunks to work on this. But the very next evening, when Josh is hanging out with other counselors, he notices two of them cursing a lot themselves.

Challenge: What advice would you give to Josh?

It's not always comfortable to be a leader, especially when you didn't sign up to be a role model. We're not expected to be 100 percent perfect. And that's the beauty of learning and leading.

Jewish Bright Spot

Rabbi Mordecai M. Kaplan (1881–1983), the founder of the Reconstructionist movement, reminds us that role modeling can go even beyond our own lifetime: "It is true that we are thrust into a world we did not make. But who makes the world into which our children are thrust?" We inherit a world from others, and we also create a world for others after us to inherit.

1. What do you think Rabbi Kaplan means by this?

2. We inherit worlds and we pass down worlds. How would you describe the world you inherited?

3. How would you describe the world you want to pass down to the next generation?

IMAGINING YOUR FUTURE: WRITING A PERSONAL VISION STATEMENT

Some people seem to know what they want in life and just go for it. Even as kids, they can tell you what they want to be when they grow up, where they want to live, and what they want to accomplish. They seem to write the future for themselves. Most of us, though, are less certain about our future, and our plans may change for many different reasons.

That doesn't mean we can't think strategically about the future, even if our plans could change. Close your eyes and summon your imagination to answer this question: Where will you be one year from now? Five years? Ten years? We can't know, but we can still dream.

Let's do some of that dreaming together right now by creating personal vision statements. A personal vision statement is a picture of ourselves in the future based on what's important to us now. It can help us think about our future based on who we want to be and what we want to contribute to the world.

Here are five guidelines for creating a meaningful personal vision statement:

1. Write it down. Writing often stimulates more intentional thinking.

2. Write it in the present tense.

3. Ensure it covers at least a few different aspects of your life: work, family, Jewish life, activities.

4. Include details that make it feel real and true to your life.

5. Keep it to one paragraph only.

For each of the following "I am" statements, peer into the future and describe where you are physically, what you're doing, who your friends are, and what's important to you.

One year from now:

I am . . .

Five years from now:

I am . . .

Ten years from now:

I am . . .

What was easiest for you about writing each vision statement? What was hardest?

Now that you've imagined your future, let's put your vision statements to work. If you're ready, try writing down three actions you can begin right now to get you closer to your personal vision.

1.

2.

3.

Jewish Bright Spot

Anne Frank (1929–1945) wrote her famous diary during the two years she and her family hid from the Nazis in the secret wing of a house in Amsterdam. She died at age fifteen in the Bergen-Belsen concentration camp, but her diary has gone on to become one of the most widely read books in the world. In it, Anne wrote, "How wonderful it is that nobody need wait a single moment before starting to improve the world."

1. What do you think inspired Anne to write this?

2. How do you think Anne's journal and dreams about her future helped her deal with the ugly realities of her life?

3. If you were to become famous for saying anything, what would it be?

Your Moral Compass: Articulating Your Leadership Values

In Lewis Carroll's book *Alice's Adventures in Wonderland*, Alice asks the Cheshire Cat, "Would you tell me, please, which way I ought to go from here?"

To which the cat responds, "That depends a good deal on where you want to get to."

Where do you want to get to? If you don't know, then any road will get you there. When we're leading, we need to know where we're going because people are following us. In the previous chapter, you created a vision for the future. Now, how do you get there?

Your values are an essential set of beliefs that describe what you stand for, keep you grounded through ambiguous or difficult times, and provide a compass for your actions and choices. When you need to make a challenging decision, you can lean into your values for guidance. A compass is only helpful, however, if you know where you want to go. So we've designed a simple compass to help you identify your unique values. If you need more room, feel free to use the space in the margins or copy this out onto a larger page.

In the top right quadrant: Write your English name, your Hebrew name, and the history of your names (if you know it).

In the top left quadrant: Write one cause that's very important to you and summarize why.

In the bottom right quadrant: Write one of your leadership goals and three of your strongest leadership skills.

In the bottom left quadrant: Write three important values you try to live by. If you're looking for values to inspire you to get started, check out the appendix, "Ten Leadership Superpowers."

Think of this compass as a way to attach your name to your strengths, a cause you care about, and some values you bring to the work. Come back to this compass any time you need direction, such as when you're facing a tough decision.

Jewish Bright Spot

In Pirkei Avot (Ethics of the Fathers), Rabbi Shimon bar Yochai praises different "crowns" of leadership—the crown of Torah, the crown of priesthood, and the crown of royalty—but concludes that "the crown of a good name is superior to them all."

1. What do you think Rabbi Shimon means by the "crown of a good name"?

2. A crown adds height and stature to the person wearing it. What have you done recently to earn the crown of a good name?

3. Rabbi Shimon implies that protecting your good name is more important than simply being a leader. What might leaders do that could tarnish their crowns?

9

LEADERSHIP BY DESIGN: WRITING YOUR PERSONAL MISSION STATEMENT

John Lennon, lead musician of "The Beatles," once said, "Life is what happens when you're busy making other plans." Most of us are so busy just living our lives that we don't always have time to think about what we are uniquely here to do. For example, Penina, now in her early twenties, from Beit Shemesh, Israel, had no intention of taking on a leadership role. She just became more and more involved in her youth movement, which eventually expanded into taking on serious responsibilities in other organizations. "I spend so much time planning for the weekend, for vacation, for college," Penina says, "for the next big thing coming up. But I've never stopped to plan what kind of leader I want to be. What kind of life I want to lead."

That's where a personal mission statement can be helpful; it can help us make plans and stay true to our values. What's the difference between a personal mission statement and the vision statement we worked on in chapter 7? A personal *vision* statement is a picture we create for ourselves of what we want to be doing at some point in the future. A personal *mission* statement is an articulation of our core values and beliefs that can help us make decisions in the here and now. It can be especially helpful when you find yourself wandering off track. If the "values compass" you created in the previous chapter helps keep you on course, you can think of your personal mission statement as a signpost along the way. We all need direction and reminders. Penina needed them to help her take a step back and decide what kind of leader she wants to be.

Mission statements are straightforward and powerful: a simple sentence or two about your values and dreams and what you most want to give the world. Don't be afraid to go big with your mission statement. Here are some personal mission statements from well-known people:

"To make people happy."
—Walt Disney

"Not merely to survive, but to thrive; and to do so with some passion, some compassion, some humor, and some style."
—Maya Angelou

"To be a teacher. And to be known for inspiring my students to be more than they thought they could be."
—Oprah Winfrey

"I shall not fear anyone on Earth. I shall fear only God. I shall not bear ill will toward anyone. I shall not submit to injustice from anyone. I shall conquer untruth by truth. And in resisting untruth, I shall put up with all suffering."
—Mahatma Gandhi

And here's one famous teen's mission statement (we met her in chapter 1):

"I want to serve the people. And I want every girl, every child, to be educated."
—Malala Yousafzai

In your personal mission statement, you may want to include more information, like:

- Your skills and talents

- Your values and dreams

- How you intend to achieve or actualize them

In his book *Lead by Greatness: How Character Can Power Your Success*, the leadership consultant Rabbi David Lapin identifies three steps that can help you discover and articulate your mission:

1. List your capabilities. These include the skills you have as well as your upbringing, education, personality, contacts, and talents.

2. Identify primary beneficiaries. These are the people you could give to most. There are many people who would be lucky to have your attention, but what are the key groups that matter to you and who can benefit from your talents?

3. Identify your passions. These are the things that energize, excite, and engage you.

Working through these three steps—what you want to do, what needs to be done, and what engages you—will help you discover your leadership sweet spot and your purpose, two important elements in crafting your personal mission statement.

Case Study

It's Michael's eighteenth birthday and his friends just left the party his parents planned for him. As he cleans up the mess and decorations, he thinks about how he'll be graduating soon, maybe voting in the next election and heading off to college. Michael always assumed that he would have accomplished more by the time he turned eighteen. He's a decent student and has good friends, but looking back, he realizes he hasn't pushed himself enough. He could have tried harder at school and socially. He could have been more involved in sports or in school clubs. Michael feels discouraged and wonders if he'll feel the same when he finishes college.

Challenge: What advice would you give to Michael?

Find a quote that really inspires you. Write or print it out and put it somewhere you can see it regularly.

Your mission statement is your road map to success. To begin, we'll use a format adapted from Laurie Beth Jones's book *The Path: Creating Your Mission Statement for Work and for Life*.

1. Circle three words in each of the following three categories—nouns, verbs, and adjectives—that you think best describe your personal mission in life. When you're done, you'll have nine words circled.

Nouns

Atmosphere	Dignity	Justice	Portal
Challenge	Education	Learner	Pursuit
Children	Embrace	Lifestyle	Quest
Citizenship	Excellence	Literacy	Religion
Commitment	Family	Love	Reverence
Community	Gift	Mastery	Safety
Compassion	Help	Mensch	Security
Concern	Home	Mitzvah	Spirituality
Culture	Integration	Opportunity	Support
Development	Judaism	Outreach	Synthesis

Verbs

Accomplish	Alleviate	Build	Communicate
Acknowledge	Appreciate	Combine	Connect
Affirm	Ascend	Commit	Construct

Verbs (continued)

Continue	Explore	Learn	Remember
Contribute	Extend	Live	Resonate
Counsel	Facilitate	Make	Safeguard
Create	Flourish	Manage	Satisfy
Defend	Fulfill	Master	Seek
Deliver	Further	Measure	Serve
Discover	Generate	Model	Share
Discuss	Give	Mold	Strive
Distribute	Grant	Motivate	Study
Dream	Heal	Negotiate	Support
Educate	Identify	Nurture	Sustain
Embody	Imbue	Open	Synthesize
Embrace	Implement	Organize	Team
Encourage	Improve	Participate	Transmit
Endeavor	Inform	Prepare	Understand
Endow	Inspire	Produce	Utilize
Engage	Instill	Progress	Validate
Enhance	Integrate	Promote	Value
Enlist	Involve	Pursue	Volunteer
Ensure	Know	Realize	Work
Experience	Lead	Relate	

Adjectives

Active	Educational	Informed	Principled
Caring	Excellent	Intellectual	Religious
Committed	Exemplary	Jewish	Responsible
Communal	Fortunate	Just	Righteous
Compassionate	Friendly	Living	Safe
Comprehensive	Giving	Loving	Warm
Creative	Happy	Modern	Welcoming
Determined	Helpful	Nurturing	Well-educated
Dignified	Inclusive	Passionate	

2. Using the words you circled, write one paragraph of no more than fifty words about your personal life mission. The shorter, the better. For example, you may want to reduce the three words in each category to one single word in each category. An effective mission statement appeals to the head, heart, and hands—your brain, your feelings, and your commitment to action.

3. Now try to get your mission statement down to twenty-five words or fewer:

The words we use and write have weight. You might want to place your mission statement where you can see it regularly, such as in a wallet or on the wall next to where you study or sleep. Howard Finger, the author of *The Mindful Entrepreneur*, for example, summarizes his as "To create the greatest sustainable value—no excuses."

On Friday night, in synagogues around the world, we welcome Shabbat with the song "Lecha Dodi," composed by Shlomo Halevi Alkabetz in the sixteenth century. One of its verses refers to Shabbat as the pinnacle of creation: "Last made, but first planned." This also seems like a deep insight into strategic planning: before you act, think about where you want to end up.

1. What does this line mean to you?

2. Why would that be included in a prayer on Shabbat?

3. Where in your leadership might this apply?

10

LEADERSHIP AND TIME MANAGEMENT

"I'm bad at time management," sixteen-year-old Zachary told us. "Sometimes I have so much work. At other times, I have too little. . . . I have times when I say yes to a lot of things and have no time, and one area will suffer." But when that happens, he starts holding back and saying no, and then he ends up bored, with too much free time on his hands.

Zachary's time trap is normal. Most of us have trouble finding the right balance between being too busy and not having enough to do. And remember, in the Torah, even God practices time management, creating the world over seven days and marking the end of each stage by counting: "And it was morning and it was evening the first day . . . the second day . . ." Even God didn't create everything in a day. But each day, God saw that "it was good."

Time management isn't just about wearing a watch or checking the time every few minutes. It's about choosing your priorities and then following through.

Inner Workout

- Do you usually set goals for yourself? If so, how? If not, why not?

- Do you usually achieve the goals you set for yourself?

- What can you do to help set goals more effectively?

Rabbi Dena Shaffer, who has made a career out of working with and engaging teens, says time management is really a matter of figuring out your priorities. "People will respect you when you set boundaries. It's okay to do so. It's a sign of your maturity and responsibility. Time management is about choices."

Some young leaders we interviewed told us they wasted too much time on social drama, social media, video games, or online shopping. Many also found time management hard because they were struggling with one oversized word: PROCRASTINATION.

Henry told us that in tenth grade he had a really "bad case" of putting off his work until later. Sometimes later turned into never. He found excuses not to open his homework: gaming, his friends, his siblings. "I was bad with procrastination but have gotten better over the past year. I just told myself the work has to get done. I just want to get it over with to lighten up my stress, and it works." If we don't manage time, it manages us.

Five Reasons We Procrastinate

1. We're not good at what we're doing (or *think* we're not).
2. We don't know where to start so we don't start at all.
3. We're waiting for the right mood, but we're never in it.
4. We're afraid to fail.
5. We're afraid to be successful because then we'll get more work.

Name Three Reasons You Procrastinate

1. _____
2. _____
3. _____

- Are you more likely to call yourself a procrastinator or a workaholic? Or neither? Or both? Why do you think that is?

- Do you spend time working on what's important or what's urgent? When you are forced to choose between the two, which do you choose?

- What do you do to relax and create balance in a busy day?

Here are some time management hacks you can try:

1. Write down what will happen if you don't do the task in front of you.

2. Find an accountability partner—someone who will keep tabs on you and vice versa.

3. Break down one job into lots of little jobs and check off each one as you do it.

Want to know where all your time goes? Try logging your time for three days in a row. You can do that by charting each hour you're awake—and blocking off your sleep time—then describe your activities in each hour. Once you're finished, fill in how long you spent doing each thing:

- Eating:
- School:
- Extra-curricular activities:
- Time with friends:

- Time with family: _____
- Homework: _____
- Exercise: _____
- Other (explain): _____

Jewish Bright Spot

One of the ways Judaism teaches us time management is by showing us that we should make time to stop. In the Torah, God's power week of creation was followed by a very intentional period of rest: "On the seventh day God finished the work that God had been doing, and God ceased on the seventh day from all the work that God had done. And God blessed the seventh day and declared it holy, because on it God ceased from all the work of creation that God had done." (Genesis 2:2–3)

1. Why does God rest in the story of creation?

2. Shabbat allows us to stop and see our work and bless it. Name a blessing in your leadership.

3. What is the most restful thing you do?

11

Leading as an Introvert, Extrovert, or Ambivert

Some of us love working behind the scenes, meeting and talking with others one on one.

Some of us love to get on a stage, pick up a mic, and fire up a crowd.

Both types of leaders are necessary.

Introverts may find that their best way to contribute as a leader is through event planning, logistical work, and small-group planning. Extroverts can be great recruiters and connectors with the capacity to inspire others. And then there are ambiverts, who are outgoing in certain settings and prefer their own company at other times.

Michelle Shapiro Abraham, a veteran educator and mentor to many youth leaders and camp programs through NFTY (National Federation of Temple Youth), the Reform Jewish youth movement, says extroverted leaders are great at "leading discussions, mobilizing people. They have a passion for certain ideas and quickly coming up with solutions." Here are her four pearls of advice for extroverts in leadership roles:

1. Be excited about your growth and be reflective.

2. Practice pulling yourself back out of the space.

3. Recognize that you may think you know what people want *but you don't actually know* unless you ask.

4. Allow what others tell you to change the way you think and act.

Introverts are essential to run any type of program, event, and organization. According to Rebecca Weisman of the United Synagogue for Conservative Judaism, who has worked for schools, congregations, youth movements, and nonprofits, "Introverts are not standing on the table and belting out songs at the top of their lungs. But leadership doesn't always happen from the person with high energy and a mind that's racing a hundred miles an hour." Instead, she suggests that adults working with teens carefully match what a project needs with the teen talent they have instead of always choosing the same people. She also suggests setting up teens for success by leveraging what teens feel good and strong about. That requires the adult to really listen and ask questions. Make sure you are as clear as you can be in the process to maximize the opportunity.

Inner Workout

Each of us is more introverted or extroverted depending on the context. For each of the settings below, place a dot where you fall on each line between *introvert* and *extrovert*.

- At school:

introvert ⟵————————————————⟶ *extrovert*

- With friends:

introvert ⟵————————————————⟶ *extrovert*

- With family:

introvert ⟵————————————————⟶ *extrovert*

- In leadership roles:

introvert ⟵————————————————⟶ *extrovert*

What did you discover about yourself after placing your dots?

Misha, sixteen, surprised himself by stepping up to lead a school club after watching a TV show about people who said yes to random opportunities like traveling or eating with strangers. When he was younger, he says, "I was frankly scared to go to my next-door neighbors to ask for a cup of milk. I'd ask my younger brother to do it." Watching the TV show, however, he noticed that something interesting always happened—and that transformed his outlook: "Why not just say yes, because something organically beautiful can come out of it. Maybe you'll meet your new best friend or a girlfriend or a role model." He says if he could design a perfect leader, it would be a hybrid of an introvert and an extrovert.

Inner Workout

- In what situations do you act more extroverted, and when do you act more introverted?

- Are you more energized by being with other people or by being alone?

Susan Cain describes herself as the "chief revolutionary" of the Quiet Revolution, a movement championing introverts. She's written two books about what she calls "quiet brilliance." The most common misunderstanding about personality type, Cain writes in *Quiet: The Power of Introverts in a World That Can't Stop Talking*, is that "introverts are antisocial and extroverts are pro-social . . . neither formulation is correct; introverts and extroverts are differently social."

Extroverts, for instance, are usually nourished by being with other people. Cain says extroverts often find themselves in an emotional state she refers to as "buzz," a rush of energized, enthusiastic feelings. To help them translate that into leadership, she recommends that they make the most of those strong emotions by building things, inspiring others, and thinking big. Cain would probably consider Rebecca, seventeen, an extroverted leader. Rebecca loves the excitement of large events, such as a large teen climate change conference where she enjoyed making the case to possible new recruits, raising money, and helping organize a summit event where teens met and spoke with US senators.

Where Rebecca struggled was with studying all the policy issues to keep well informed. For help in this area, she worked with some teen leaders who'd probably consider themselves introverts. Theses friends were more comfortable writing scripts and staying behind the scenes to help their teams prepare.

Introverts usually prefer less stimulation and often feel nourished by being alone. Cain believes that while we may think of extroverts as better leaders, introverted leaders can unquestionably deliver wonderful outcomes. "The ranks of transformative leaders in history illustrate this," she writes. "Gandhi, Eleanor Roosevelt, and Rosa Parks were all introverts."

Avital describes herself as a quiet person who resented being overlooked for other types of leadership roles even though she always showed up to lead youth services at her synagogue. She finally decided to take the initiative and sign herself up for a more official leadership role. When others assume you lack leadership skills because you are quiet, Avital worries that "it can lead to a loss of self-confidence, an inability to develop certain skills, and the loss of a voice in the room."

Ian Kandel began his leadership journey as an introverted teen and jokes that he still prefers to be backstage, next to the sound engineers. He grew up in his local youth movement, which led him to take on larger roles, first as regional president and then leading organizations and student government at the George Washington University. "I don't seek the attention; I love responsibility," he says. Today, he is with BBYO, working to reinvent the concept of the youth group for today's teens. His take on leadership is slightly different; he believes good leaders are also good followers. "What makes a successful movement is not any one person. It's being one of the first followers." From experience he has learned that you can be a good leader on one project or in one group or organization and a good follower in another.

Introvert. Extrovert. Ambivert. Never be afraid to bring who you are into how you lead.

Rabbi David Bashevkin, the director of education of NCSY (National Conference of Synagogue Youth) and founder of the new media company 18Forty, recognizes that different personality types also have different spiritual needs: "Not everyone has the same orientation to religiosity and spirituality. We need doors with flashing lights and fireworks, but we also need a doorway that's a lot quieter, that's filled with conversations and ideas." He relates these two kinds of doors to the giving of the Ten Commandments and, not long afterward, the creation of a golden calf. Rabbi Bashevkin says this of the giving of the commandments to the ancient Israelites: "They were given with lightning, thunder, drama, and a sensationalism that we most associate with teen events. That set of tablets was smashed. . . . The second set of tablets was absent the noise; they were created more quietly, organically from the people. Long-term religious growth also has to prize interiority."

1. Imagine being at Mount Sinai. Do you think you would have felt fear or awe? When you think of your own spirituality, what appeals more— boisterous community events or the quiet of prayer and conversation?

2. In your own leadership activities, how do you make space for those who are not like you?

12

WHAT IS STRESS?

So you're the head of the tenth-grade student council *and* you're running a car wash in a few hours *and* the hose just broke.

and you have a huge math test tomorrow (it's your worst subject)

and your best friend complains that you're never around anymore

and you have a project due

and you went to sleep last night at 1:30 a.m.—that's technically this morning

and tomorrow you've got to do all this again.

When does the fun begin?

When we take on too many leadership roles and feel overwhelmed, it's probably time for a stress check. Listen to what your body is telling you. Are all the things you're doing really making you happy? Even if you like every project and commitment on its own, when you lump them all together, do they add up to too much? Stress is like treading water. Most of us can manage it for a few minutes but not day after day without an end in sight.

Stress is how our bodies respond to physical, mental, or emotional pressure. It changes our chemical balance. It can raise our adrenaline and cortisol and increase our heart rate. Stress can also lead to moodiness, headaches, stomach cramps, acne, rashes, and sleep loss.

Stress can make it hard to focus or concentrate. It serves a useful function when it alerts us to danger and to places, people, and situations to avoid. But it can also make it more difficult to cope with an overwhelming situation. If we experience too much stress, it can spiral into a type of anxiety that can make us feel sad, incapable, or incompetent.

When Hannah was in high school, she had board meetings for her organization twice a week, dance and piano lessons, standardized exams, and a lot of homework to do. She felt that she had spread herself too thin and was doing nothing right. She would put five things on her to-do list, get only two done, and then feel terrible about herself. She says, "I've been overcommitted my whole life. I think I needed guidance on where I should be spending my time."

Hannah was too busy to do a good job at anything: school, extracurricular activities, and her leadership role with her local youth movement. She got frustrated with her advisor because they could not see eye to eye, and her teachers and advisor were frustrated with her. She needed help but didn't want to ask for it. By the time Hannah reached twelfth grade, she didn't want to do anything anymore—not her schoolwork, not her leadership commitments, not her volunteering.

Hannah says that when things got overwhelming, some teens she knew turned to smoking, drinking, drugs, unhealthy relationships, gaming, or just escaping online—all things that may numb the tension temporarily but cannot take it away.

In the Bible, Queen Esther—another young leader, since some believe she was only fourteen when she met King Ahasuerus—faced an enormous challenge: saving her people from destruction. The story tells us that she was "greatly agitated." How could she not be? She was young and powerless. Her people's future was at stake. She was defying death to break the king's rules. Talmudic sages describe various physical symptoms of distress that Esther might have experienced under all this pressure.

But Mordechai, her uncle, needed her to know that this was her time to shine. He sent her a message pointing out that while everything depended on her, "Who knows whether it was for just such a time as this that you came into your royal position!" (Esther 4:14)

That gave Esther the boost she needed to lean into her fear rather than giving in to it. She realized that she had a higher purpose. That gave her the strength to manage the fear and the stress, find her focus and her leadership voice, and eventually redeem her people.

When you're in a leadership role, you deserve to feel capable, confident, and competent. Stress gets in the way of those feelings. Stress is real. But you're not helpless in combating it. Here are a few tried and tested things you can do for genuine relief—and each begins with a question.

1. Will this challenge make you stronger?

If you're feeling stressed, you're not alone. Dr. Betsy Stone, a psychologist and consultant who has worked with teens for decades, says this is the most anxious generation she's ever encountered. "I think our kids are more anxious because they've been told they should be happy. Unhappiness is a stress that can help people grow. When I have resilience, I have self-esteem. I have faced a dragon and not been defeated."

2. What inspires you to be stronger?

As we suggested in chapter 9, when we were crafting your personal mission statement, take a quote that makes you feel strong and print it out, put it somewhere you can see it regularly, or use it as wallpaper on your phone. Read it when you need it.

3. Can you ride this wave?

Each of us has a reservoir of happy times to draw on when we're down. We cycle in and out of emotions—positive and negative—so if you can, try to ride the wave until things calm down. Remember: how you feel now is *not* how you will always feel. Don't convince yourself that every breakup or bad test grade is the end of the world.

4. Can you describe the problem precisely?

When things are going wrong, we tend to "catastrophize," exaggerate and tell ourselves it's much worse than it actually is. If everything is terrible or wonderful, life becomes too extreme to manage well, so it can be helpful to sit down and put it into perspective.

'If I don't finish my homework, I will be kicked out of school.'

'I need to finish my homework or I will get a lower grade in this class.'

5. Can you name what's working well?

Reminding ourselves of our blessings can help put challenges into perspective. This doesn't make problems disappear, but it can make them smaller. Try to find one thing that is working for each thing that isn't.

6. Can you stay in the present?

When we catastrophize, we imagine things are not only bad now but will get much worse in the future. Why go there when we don't know what the future holds? There's enough work to do now. It's best to be wide awake in the moment. We don't have to live life in the emergency lane all the time.

My Blessed-Not-Stressed List

1.

2.

3.

4.

5.

7. Are you doing too much at one time?

Stress often comes with taking on too many tasks at the same time and then feeling as if you're doing badly at each one. Try doing one thing at a time rather than multitasking. When you're studying, study. When you're with friends, be there totally. When you're leading, lead. Be present.

8. Do you know how amazing you are?

The goal isn't to be perfect because there is no perfect. If you can't do it 100 percent right, it's still worth doing. What would your life look and feel like if you believed you were good enough? Because you are.

9. Where can you get help?

If you're experiencing stress that does not let up or you find yourself feeling very sad, confused, and nervous without an end in sight, it's probably time to get professional help. You don't have to carry this alone. Speak to your parents, your school counselor, or a therapist. There are many effective techniques to help you manage the overload. Don't be afraid to ask for help.

- Name three responsibilities that stress you out:

1.

2.

3.

- Would cutting out one of the nonessential commitments reduce stress? Why or why not?

- Describe some of the ways you feel stress in your body.

Is there any activity or leadership role you took on because of pressure, guilt, or to build up your college résumé? Dr. Stone says, "We spend our lives building résumés as opposed to building character." Is there something you can let go of to do the work that really moves you?

Hannah, who we met earlier in this chapter, eventually figured out that the best way for her to manage stress was to stop, pause whatever she was doing, listen to her symptoms, talk through her feelings, evaluate next steps, and then—and only then—decide how to respond. She recognized that she could only manage stress by slowing everything down and thinking more carefully about what she agreed to—or didn't.

Over time, with a long break and with lots of help, Hannah took on fewer leadership responsibilities and limited herself to working on issues she genuinely cared about. Her stress levels went way down. Hannah got out of the fast lane by learning to do what she loved—and started to love what she was doing. And when you love what you're doing, it's a lot easier to lead.

So take a deep breath . . .

Jewish Bright Spot

A biblical proverb teaches that "if there is anxiety in a person's mind let them quash it, and turn it into joy with a good word." (Proverbs 12:25) The sages of the Talmud interpreted this verse in an unusual way, as an invitation to speak about problems: "If there is anxiety in a person's mind, talk it through and turn it into the joy of a good word."

1. What do you think this verse means?

2. Describe a time when talking through a stressful situation brought relief and clarity.

3. This verse moves quickly from anxiety to joy. What "good word" would do that for you?

13

GRIT AND RESILIENCE: THE STRENGTH TO KEEP LEADING

When Hillel's basketball team isn't doing well, they look to him as captain. "You need to be strong-willed to lead," he says. "A leader grows through a lot of adversity, and you need to be the toughest one in the pack." So even when he's feeling low, he reminds his players, "Hey, we're going to get through this. Let's keep our heads up." Picking yourself up when you're losing is hard in sports—and essential for good leadership.

Case Study

Ashley is the captain of her high school debate team. They are halfway through a big tournament against a rival school. Her team is losing—by a lot. Team members are grumbling that they may as well quit now instead of losing . . . again. They complain that they are tired and that their training was a waste of time. Ashley feels the exhaustion of losing creep up on her as well. But as the captain, she puts on a determined face and huddles with them for a pep talk. They still lose. Then in the hallway after the debate, she overhears some members openly questioning her ability to lead. Debate season is just beginning.

Challenge: What advice would you give to Ashley to help her respond?

Teaching in inner-city public schools, the neuroscientist Dr. Angela Duckworth noticed that the students who tended to succeed were not necessarily the brightest but those who stayed the course; those who failed and stood up again and again. She went on to study psychology and write about this quality, which she refers to as "grit": a combination of passion and perseverance for a singularly important goal. "As much as talent counts, effort counts twice," she writes.

For Dr. Duckworth, grit means staying with problems longer and dusting off rejection. She says that one thing people with grit often have in common is that they don't overreact to setbacks and failures, as hard as that can be.

Inner Workout

- Describe a leadership situation you were in where you gave up or experienced rejection.

- Describe a leadership situation where you picked yourself up after facing defeat.

- What helps inspire you when your energy and motivation are low?

Abby is an example of a teen with talent *and* grit. When she attempted to run a cooking class for kids with disabilities, she admits she did a bad job initially. The kitchen was hectic; the atmosphere was tense. "Parents let me know I wasn't doing a good job."

The kids were frustrated, the parents were frustrated, and Abby was frustrated, too. She was almost ready to give up . . . but she didn't. "I went home and thought about how to make it work." She experimented with more kid-friendly recipes and found ways to get the kids more involved in her cooking demonstrations. "At the end of the summer, I was recognized by the parents for my skills of inclusion."

By shifting her behavior, Abby discovered that grit is not about bouncing back; it's about bouncing *forward*. Abby used her mistakes to become even better at managing than she was before. As a leader, you aren't going to be perfect or liked 100 percent of the time. Grit gives us the strength to face that reality and do what needs to be done to achieve a better outcome. That's leadership!

In the Torah, Jacob was in grave danger from his brother Esau. Fleeing, he encountered a man who wrestled with him. Jacob ended up bruised and severely injured. The man was about to leave, but Jacob held him tightly and demanded a blessing. This seems strange. Why did Jacob hold on to his opponent instead of running away? Maybe he recognized that even the most difficult situations can provide a blessing. They make us stronger and more mature. Our challenges shape us and make us who we are. They give us grit.

After wrestling with the angel, Jacob was renamed Israel, the name of our people and our country, from a word meaning "to struggle": "For you wrestled with God and humans and prevailed." (Genesis 32:29) Built into the DNA of the name Israel is the capacity for grit and resilience.

Inner Workout

- Describe a situation where you needed more grit than you thought you had.

- When is the last time you praised someone else for having grit?

- What's the nicest compliment you ever received as a leader? Don't be afraid to say it.

Grit doesn't necessarily mean sticking with something you really don't want to do. For Abby, success required her to tap into why she wanted to offer her cooking program in the first place: empowering kids by helping them create delicious treats. As Dr. Duckworth explains, "Grit is about working on something you care about so much that you're willing to stay loyal to it . . . it's doing what you love, but not just falling in love—staying in love."

One of the ways Abby built up her confidence as a leader was holding on to compliments: "Any time I get a compliment it keeps me going, even if it's small. When you get rewarded for leading, it makes you want to lead more." And on those days when no one has a good word, Abby has a solution: "Sometimes you have to tell yourself you did a good job."

That's grit!

Jewish Bright Spot

A biblical proverb reminds us of the power of grit: "The righteous person falls seven times and gets up." (Proverbs 24:16)

1. Why do you think this proverb uses a large number like seven?

2. What place does grit have in your spiritual life?

3. Think of a time you had to get up multiple times from an emotional fall. What did you learn from it and how did it change you?

14

MAKING BETTER DECISIONS

Ari has leadership roles on his cross-country and track teams and worked as a counselor-in-training at a camp. In his personal life he's made many major decisions, such as asking his parents to send him to a Jewish high school, a decision he's proud of. And he's learned that leadership, too, involves a lot of decision-making. "I usually make the right decision," Ari told us. "Probably." He didn't sound so sure.

When Ari's decisions have positive results, he feels proud. When a very young camper in his bunk wanted to climb the rock wall, only to get scared and start to cry when he was halfway up, Ari had to decide: Encourage the boy to continue climbing up or help him get down? By the time Ari reached him, the camper was so tired that he couldn't climb down. Ari put his arms around the crying boy, who still desperately wanted to get to the top. Although Ari could have persuaded him to change his mind, he chose to help the boy achieve his goal instead: "I coached him step by step, and after ten minutes, he finally got to the top. He smiled really wide. I was super-excited for him. It was a special moment for me."

But not every decision is a winner, as Ari has discovered the hard way:

> There are times I make bad decisions. I have to live with that and learn from them. I might think a decision is right at the time and later will look back on it and say, "That wasn't a good idea," and consider what else I could have done.

- Do you think of yourself as a good decision-maker? Why or why not?

- Once you've made a decision, do you second-guess yourself? Give an example here.

- What's a big decision you must make soon and what factors are you weighing?

A Good Decision Quiz

Rate your decision-making abilities. For each of the following seven aspects of decision-making, give yourself a score from 1 to 10 for how well you do at each aspect.

When you must make a decision, do you . . .

- Weigh the benefits and the drawbacks? _____
- Think about short-term and long-term consequences? _____
- Understand the rational and emotional aspects of the decision? _____
- Think about who else will be affected by the decision and how? _____
- Set a deadline? _____
- Take responsibility for the decision you made? _____
- Own your mistakes? _____

Have a look at the scores you just gave yourself. What did you learn about yourself? What are you proud of and what areas could benefit from a different approach? Ari learned that making good decisions helped propel him forward: "If you want to get something done, you have to see the goal and go out and get it rather than waiting for it to come to you." Going after your dreams starts with making decisions.

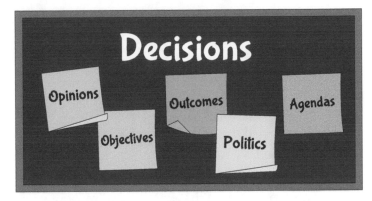

Jewish Bright Spot

There is a phrase that appears in the Talmud several times that presents one approach to decision-making. "Certainty or doubt? Go with the certainty."

1. What is the merit of this advice?

2. What is the problem with this advice?

3. Think about a decision you have to make. What are you certain about and what are the risks?

15

LIMITING CHOICES

Making choices is an important part of establishing independence. When our right to make choices for ourselves is taken away, we feel (justifiably) frustrated. But when we have too many choices, we can feel overwhelmed. Go into any supermarket and you'll find an entire aisle of shampoo. How much time do you want to spend on that choice? Professor of social theory and action Dr. Barry Schwartz refers to this as the "paradox of choice." Overloaded with too many choices, which we think we ought to enjoy, we instead become unhappy and less able to decide. "At this point, choice no longer liberates, but debilitates," he writes in *The Paradox of Choice: Why More Is Less*.

Finding the sweet spot where you feel empowered and not overcome with doubt is part of great leadership. That comes with making the choice to limit your choices.

Inner Workout

- If you could change one aspect of the way you make decisions, what would it be?

- Describe the way you handled a leadership decision that did not work out the way you wanted it to.

- Name a decision you had to make where you had too many options. What happened?

Is there a good method to narrow down your choices so you can make the best possible decision more efficiently? We think so. We scanned the research, read what experts had to say, and came up with these suggestions:

- Instead of saying, "Should I do this *or* that?" see if you can find a way to do this *and* that.

- Reduce your choices to three options.

- Make a pro-and-con list but know that not every pro or con matters to the same degree.

- Talk over your decision with two wise people in your life. Talking to too many people can make things *more* confusing, not less.

- Become a "satisficer," a word Dr. Schwartz uses to describe when you "settle for something that is good enough and don't worry about the possibility that there might be something better."

- Get all the information you need, then do something super relaxing to give your brain a break. This helps your intuition work better.

- Know that most decisions can be undone. That does not mean there won't be consequences, but it lets us own our mistakes and press the "redo" button if we must.

- Embrace the business journalist Suzy Welch's "10-10-10 rule": ask yourself what the impact of your decision will be ten minutes from now, ten months from now, and ten years from now.

The Talmudic expression "There is no happiness like the resolution of doubt" reminds us that resolving doubts liberates us and that freedom and self-knowledge, in turn, make us happy. So who are we? Our decisions help us figure that out.

Jewish Bright Spot

Praying is one way we express our deepest yearnings. In the Amidah (Standing Prayer), we ask God to give us intelligence, insight, and perception: "You favor humans with perception and teach humankind understanding. Grant us from Your perception, understanding, and intellect. Blessed are You, God, Who grants perception."

1. Why do people pray for wisdom?

2. Have you ever prayed to make a good decision? Describe that moment.

3. Write a prayer of no more than three sentences about an important decision you have in front of you.

LEADING OTHERS

If I am only for myself, what am I?

כְּשֶׁאֲנִי לְעַצְמִי, מָה אֲנִי?

U'kh'she'ani le'atzmi, mah ani?

(Pirkei Avot 1:14)

16

Leading the Flock

In the Torah, shepherding can often be a path to leadership. From Abel to Abraham, from Rachel to Moses, King David and beyond, so many of ancient Israel's leaders were shepherds. Think of it as the MBA of their time. In Psalm 23, even God is described as a shepherd: "Adonai is my shepherd; I lack nothing." When leaders care for us the way shepherds care for their flock—protecting, nurturing, and guiding—we can grow in safety and security. We are not afraid.

As we open this section on working with others, let's dig deeper and explore why shepherding is such a good metaphor for leadership. Shepherds . . .

- Pay constant attention to the needs of their flock.

- Nurture their flock, especially the stragglers, and anticipate their future needs.

- Protect their flock from predators and threats.

- Create movement forward, motivating their flock to look for new places to graze.

- Adapt to changing weather conditions, landscape, and terrain.

- Are comfortable being alone and communing with God and nature.

- Know that they do not speak the same language as their flock but can lead them anyway.

One more thing: shepherds don't stand in front of their flock; they lead from behind. This gives them a great advantage. Similarly, we may believe that great leaders lead from the front, but by leading from the back, leaders can often be far more effective.

- Describe a "shepherding" moment in your leadership.

- When have you been a member of a flock and led with care by someone else?

- Describe a time when your most effective leadership came from being in the back of a room and not the front.

Here are a few ideas to help you improve your shepherding skills right now with those you lead:

- **Mind the stragglers.** Identify a few people who are on the margins of your team or group and who might benefit from more of your attention. How can you listen to their needs and reach out?

- **Grow the flock.** Make a list, by yourself or with help, of people you'd love to get involved with your cause or organization. Then invite them to join you.

- **Pay attention.** Name a challenge your group is facing and create time to listen and understand what may be going on for individual members.

Only one verse in the Torah shows Moses shepherding his flock. As he is out looking after his sheep, he experiences a moment of wonder:

> Now Moses . . . drove the flock into the wilderness, and came to Horeb, the mountain of God. An angel of Adonai appeared to him in a blazing fire out of a bush. He gazed, and there was a bush all aflame, yet the bush was not consumed. Moses said, "I must turn aside to look at this marvelous sight; why doesn't the bush burn up?" When Adonai saw that he had turned aside to look, God called to him out of the bush: "Moses! Moses!" He answered, "Here I am." (Exodus 3:1–4)

1. What in Moses's behavior here makes God call out to him?

2. Why might God have chosen a burning bush as a symbol of leadership?

3. Have you ever had a moment of wonder that changed your life?

The Power of Empathy

Rachel spent three summers volunteering in Israeli residential-care settings for children. Some were orphanages; others were respite homes for foster children, at-risk youth, and children who had experienced abuse. Children in these situations are often afraid to form new relationships because they've been let down many times. But Rachel was able to reach them because she has empathy—the ability to look outside herself to think about what "her kids," as she calls them, have suffered and what they need to thrive.

Empathy means understanding someone else from their own perspective. It involves imagining the emotions they might be feeling, based on our own experiences, and then using that knowledge to connect and bond with others without judgment. The Torah encourages empathy when it tells us thirty-six times not to mistreat strangers because we were strangers in Egypt. Instead of forgetting about the pain, we are told to lean into it and allow that suffering to teach us to relieve the pain of others.

Having empathy is often the beginning of leadership. Moses's first act of leadership was prompted by empathy. He looked and saw an Egyptian taskmaster beating a Jewish slave. Moses was not a slave himself, but he observed the exploitation of slaves around him, understood their pain, and resolved to do something about it. Thousands of years later, Moses's challenge to Pharaoh, "Let my people go," remains a motto of social justice.

How can we become more empathetic leaders? One way is to make ourselves smaller so that others can grow and develop. Rachel eventually became part of the leadership team that ran summer camps at a large orphanage. As she became responsible for training and helping other counselors, she found that she had to take herself out of the room. Even though she loved being with the children, she knew she had to make space for them to bond with their new counselors and not constantly gravitate toward her. That, too, is an expression of empathy—putting your own needs to the side to ensure that others' needs are met.

Many professionals working with teens told us that empathy is one of the key skills they look for in a leader. One professional, who started out as a teen leader herself, observed, "It takes hard work for teens to focus on others, but if they can't, they will never lead well."

Case Study

Aviv is the head of student council. She is supposed to speak to the school board tomorrow night, and many students are counting on her to push back on some major changes the school wants to make. She has prepared her remarks and practiced them. But then her dad starts having intense chest pain, and he's rushed to the hospital. Crying, nervous, and unable to concentrate on anything other than her father's health, Aviv texts Rami, her VP, and asks him to give the presentation. He agrees and calls her to find out what he is supposed to do. Rami hears Aviv crying on the phone but says nothing. Aviv hangs up, angry. She then sends him a text saying she doesn't want a heartless person representing student council.

Challenge: What advice would you give to Rami?

Being empathetic comes naturally to some people; others find they need to work harder to achieve it.

Rachel knows where her empathy comes from: "My proudest leadership accomplishment is that I'm the oldest of six children!" Understanding and managing her siblings helped her be more empathetic: "Psychologically, I grew up as the leader of the pack in terms of my place in the family," Rachel explains. "Sometimes my only job is to clean up the garbage and set the example. You don't have to be the oldest child, or a politician, or the head of your class. You can wake up any day and take action."

- Where are you in the birth order of your family? Do you think it has influenced your leadership?

- Describe a moment of empathy that transformed into a leadership role.

- Have you ever felt compassion fatigue, when you're so emotionally and physically exhausted by showing empathy or caring for others that it becomes hard to lead?

Rachel sees leadership as a true calling; she's inspired to do all she does, in part, by her desire to serve God and represent the Jewish people. She has learned that having empathy means communicating honestly and gently. "To be a leader," she says, "you need to be straightforward without being forceful. There's a difference."

Leadership starts the moment you can really see someone else and respond in a way that shows you understand what they're going through: "Be yourself but step out of your comfort zone a little bit," Rachel reminds us. "Small-scale leadership is seeing a kid sitting alone and reaching out to them." Empathy is all about seeing the needs of another, trying to understand those needs, and sharing the burden even in some small way.

Jewish Bright Spot

At the Passover seder, many of the foods we eat could be called "empathy foods." Salt water reminds us of tears; *charoset* reminds us of the mortar we used to make bricks; *maror* speaks to the bitterness of slavery, and matzah is both the bread of affliction, reminding us of those painful years, and the bread of freedom, since we made it on our way out of Egypt. In the haggadah, we read these famous words: "In each and every generation, we are obligated to see ourselves *as if we personally went out from Egypt . . .*"

1. Why are we asked to reexperience slavery?

2. What could you add to the seder to enhance your personal connection to this period of Jewish history?

3. Can you think of an "empathy food" in your life?

18

THE LOST ART OF LISTENING

In the previous chapter, we discussed empathy—focusing on meeting the needs of others. If we don't know what someone else needs, we can't lead. Listening is one way to understand what others need, making this one of the most important dimensions of leadership. You may have heard that we have two ears and one mouth so that we can listen twice as much as we speak. But that doesn't always happen. For most of us, good listening doesn't come naturally; it has to be learned. Different situations demand different kinds of listening.

Inner Workout

- Name a person you consider to be a good listener. What do they do when you speak to make sure you feel heard?

- In what situations do you find yourself listening attentively, and what makes you tune out?

- What's one thing you could do right now to improve your listening?

Listening well takes time, along with the discipline to hold back until the other person is finished speaking. Maybe you've even been in a situation where someone was so eager to connect with what you had to say that they didn't even let you finish your sentence.

In our desire to share an idea, build on what another person has said, or share that we've had a similar experience, we sometimes interrupt. We may "get" what they're saying, but we're not listening well, and if we can't listen, focus, and respect that person's unique experience, it's going to push them away. Listening is hard work.

Challenge yourself to become a better listener by waiting until someone has finished speaking before you respond. What are three ways you can remind yourself to hold off on speaking until they're done?

1.

2.

3.

Here are four different listening strategies. Some of these may come more naturally to you; others may be more challenging.

- **Active listening.** Use body language such as eye contact, nodding, or gesturing with your hands to show you're listening. When the person stops speaking, repeat part of what you've heard to keep the focus on them. This creates empathy. Active listening is especially important when responding to criticism. Becoming defensive can shut someone else down and make them feel it's not safe to share their experience.

  Example:

  JOEY: I had such a rough math test this afternoon.

  SAMANTHA: Yeah, I bet I failed my history test.

  Better, more active response from **SAMANTHA:** That sounds hard.

- **Mirroring.** Mirroring involves repeating the last word (or the last few words) with a question mark when there's a pause. This makes the speaker feel heard. It also encourages them to go deeper into a specific point.

  Example:

  JOEY: I had such a rough math test this afternoon.

  SAMANTHA: Rough test?

  JOEY: Yeah, I really wasn't prepared.

  SAMANTHA: Prepared?

  JOEY: I had so much to do last week that I didn't prioritize it.

- **Checking in.** If someone says something you disagree with, take a second to make sure you've understood what they're saying before you respond. The more specific, the better.

  Example:

  JOEY: I had such a rough math test this afternoon. I totally blew it. I really wish you'd have shared your answers with me. I really needed a good grade on this for the semester.

  SAMANTHA: It sounds like you're saying you would have done better had I shared my answers with you?

  JOEY: Yep, basically.

  SAMANTHA: I'm sorry about that, but you know how I feel about cheating.

- **Accountable listening.** If someone comes to you with a piece of information, advice, or a complaint, don't just respond in the moment. When you follow up later with ideas, answers, or results, people feel that they matter.

  Example:

  SAMANTHA: Joey, I know yesterday was a hard day for you because of that math test. Are you feeling better today?

Getting better at listening is a matter of practice. And because every day is usually filled with interactions—with parents, friends, teachers, siblings, and strangers—there's a lot of opportunity for practice. But it's not always easy to break out of old patterns. Sometimes it can help to experiment and see how a new approach might work and how it makes you feel. Here are a few tips to enhance your listening skills:

- Start with a check-in for accuracy: "Let me make sure I understand. You are feeling . . ."

- Stay curious—ask questions to better understand their point of view.

- Listen with your eyes—sustain eye contact so that the person you're listening to feels you are focusing on the conversation.

- Try not to cross your arms and legs so your body says you're open.

- Pay attention to how much talking you've done versus how much time you spend listening in a conversation.

- Let the other person speak first and last.

- Try not to "fix" things or offer advice if that's not what they're asking you for.

- Multitasking isn't great for listening so it's always best to put your phone away when in conversation.

When we listen profoundly, we are doing more than leading well. We are engaging in a divinely inspired act. One of Judaism's central prayers, the Shema, starts by asking us to listen: "Listen, O Israel: Adonai our God, Adonai is one." (Deuteronomy 6:4) God, too, is a listener, as we see from these verses from the book of Psalms:

- "Heed the sound of my cry, my king and God, for I pray to You. Hear my voice, O Adonai, at daybreak; at daybreak I plead before You, and wait." (Psalm 5:3–4)

- "I love that Adonai hears my voice, my pleas; for God turns God's ear to me whenever I call." (Psalm 116:1–2)

- "In my distress I called on Adonai, cried out to my God . . . God heard my voice; my cry to God reached God's ears." (Psalm 18:7)

1. Describe the way God listens in these verses.

2. Which of the four listening strategies mentioned above can you identify in the way God listens in these verses?

3. How does the person writing these verses know that God listens?

Since the Torah teaches that we are created in the image of God, we can follow in God's ways best by being engaged listeners.

19

LEADING OUTSIDE YOUR COMFORT ZONE

We all have comfort zones; the people, places, and situations with which we're familiar. But while leading within our own comfort zone may be easier, it isn't always what's best for us or for the world around us. Staying within your comfort zone could mean missing a lot of adventures—and lots of opportunities to lead.

Jon, for example, volunteered for a local chapter of a national organization that helps kids with serious illnesses. But the assignment they offered him was bigger than he'd anticipated: a boy was coming to his city for cancer treatment every three months. Would Jon be willing to take the boy out to have fun on days when he wasn't in treatment? Jon was suddenly outside his comfort zone, the place where things felt safe and certain. He had never worked this closely with a child who had cancer. Nothing seemed fun about this assignment. But he didn't say no.

In the middle box below, list three activities that feel totally within your comfort zone. In the left box, list three activities slightly outside of your comfort zone. In the right box, put three activities that feel totally outside of your comfort zone.

Dr. Betsy Stone, a psychologist and professor whose insights we've shared elsewhere in this book, has been working with teens since her own teenage years. She believes being able to connect with someone who isn't like you is a real leadership skill, and it requires you to take risks. "Leadership needs to be about creating a bridge with others," Dr. Stone says. That includes "a willingness to be vulnerable to other people's experiences and to find ways to hear and value the other without feeling that you've been diminished."

Inner Workout

- Describe a time you really went out of your comfort zone.

- What was most uncomfortable about the situation?

- What did you gain?

Jon had some genuine fears about spending time with the boy: he was facing serious illness; he had lost his hair; he had suffered in ways that Jon had not. Only after preparing himself emotionally by talking to his parents, friends, and an advisor with the organization and then spending a few days with the boy did Jon start to see him as a person and not a disease:

> We planned three insane days, and he had the greatest time. I felt so much freedom and creativity. I had the greatest time seeing him have the greatest time. This was a really sick kid, and for a while, when we were together, he wasn't feeling sick. It's hard to describe but I felt happy and fulfilled.

Jon discovered that only by getting out of his comfort zone was he able to be where the real magic happens.

We might be tempted to stay in our comfort zone because we want to be at ease and don't want to create stress for ourselves. Yet some of the most compelling and memorable experiences we have in life happen when we journey outside of our normal spaces. Think of a place you traveled to that expanded your horizons. In leadership, when we take risks, it might feel like we're on insecure ground. We risk being judged. But that may be the only way we can change anything.

Case Study

Arianna is in the middle of her term as president of her school's student council. She holds a town hall meeting to get feedback on what's working and what isn't. Only five students show up: three are her close friends; the other two show up at everything, seemingly just to criticize Arianna. They take turns at the meeting criticizing her leadership style and a number of programs she created while her three friends say nothing. An awkward silence descends. Arianna feels like when it comes to those two, there's nothing she can get right. And the job is hard enough without their complaints.

Challenge: What advice would you give to Arianna?

Jewish Bright Spot

The Talmud shares the story of Honi the Circle Maker, who received his odd name because once, during a drought, Honi drew a circle in the dust, stood inside it, and informed God that he would not move until it rained. When it began to drizzle, Honi told God that he was not satisfied and expected more rain; it then began to pour. He explained that he wanted a calm rain, at which point the rain calmed.

1. Why did Honi draw a circle and stand in it?

2. Why was he creating a "discomfort zone" for himself?

3. Rain eventually fell in great quantities because Honi created a new zone—his circle—to protest. Describe a situation where you didn't budge until you were able to change something.

20

Stop the Trash Talk

"Did you see how little that guy gave to our student council campaign, even though he drives such a nice car?"

"That girl keeps making mistakes on the court because she always makes them in life."

"If he would just dress better, our team would look better. He's so cheap when it comes to his clothes."

We hear trash talk all the time.

Now imagine you've just finished a board meeting, and out of the corner of your eye you see the student council president leaning in and whispering to the vice president while looking over critically at another board member. From his facial expression you're pretty sure he's saying something negative. Then he turns his gaze on you, still whispering. You wonder what he's saying about you. You imagine the worst, and you come away having stopped trusting him. You don't even want to go to the next meeting. Trash talking corrodes trust and kindness, and makes it difficult for people to work together to effect positive change. Gossip hurts.

Yakova, an energetic high school student who has taken on several leadership roles, from Model UN to Mock Trial, says that one of Judaism's most powerful teachings that guides her in working with others is the prohibition against *lashon hara*, speaking badly of others:

> There are a lot of times in leadership when it's really easy to start talking badly about people. Lashon hara feels damaging to me as a leader. I do my best to minimize destructive speech. You need to talk to people in a constructive way.

This kind of moral discipline is not easy. As a leader, you might have access to information about people or have negative interactions with them. You need to be trustworthy about guarding others' reputations and ensuring that they feel safe around you and can confide in you. If people don't trust you, they may have a hard time following you or putting their best efforts forward for your cause or organization. Building a relationship of trust generates positive, productive collaboration—and that trust begins with speaking well of others and avoiding conversations behind someone's back.

The Torah is pretty clear about this: "Do not go about spreading slander about your people." (Leviticus 19:16) That doesn't mean just talking badly about others; it's about going from person to person and spreading gossip (even if it's true). The emphasis on "your people" points to the way we think and talk about the people around us. As a leader, you can be part of creating a positive atmosphere and a culture of integrity for everybody around you.

When you're a Jewish leader, that sometimes means you need to stand up against something everyone else is doing. Rabbi Akiva Tatz, who trained as a physician in South Africa before studying and becoming more committed to Judaism, writes in his book *The Thinking Jewish Teenager's Guide to Life* that "Judaism requires the courage to think powerfully about values, and it requires the courage to reject values despite their acceptance by society at large."

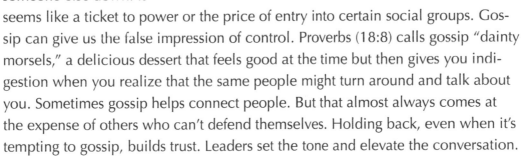

People gossip for all kinds of reasons. It can make us feel better to put someone else down. It seems like a ticket to power or the price of entry into certain social groups. Gossip can give us the false impression of control. Proverbs (18:8) calls gossip "dainty morsels," a delicious dessert that feels good at the time but then gives you indigestion when you realize that the same people might turn around and talk about you. Sometimes gossip helps connect people. But that almost always comes at the expense of others who can't defend themselves. Holding back, even when it's tempting to gossip, builds trust. Leaders set the tone and elevate the conversation.

- Describe some typical gossip you might hear when leading.

- What's a piece of gossip that hurt you?

- What's a piece of gossip you shared that may have hurt someone? (Don't worry, we won't tell anyone!)

The thing about gossip is that it never stops with one person, and it very often boomerangs back.

Exploring traditional Jewish approaches to lashon hara in his book *Words That Help, Words That Heal*, Rabbi Joseph Telushkin writes, "Words have consequences, and if you use them to hurt people, your victims will find ways to hurt you in return." Criticizing or humiliating someone in front of others, starting or spreading rumors, or believing them, can create tense work environments for leaders, adding drama that tends to end badly and distract us from the important work we have to do.

Of course, there are times when it's okay, or even essential, to share "negative truths." For example, if you are asked for a reference, Judaism allows you to speak both positively and negatively about the person, and lying about negative experiences can have serious repercussions. If you cannot be honest, acting both respectfully and fairly toward others, then you cannot be trusted.

Here's an ultimate statement of trust. Two Talmudic sages were once having a debate. One said it wasn't really lashon hara if you speak badly about a person in their presence. Another disagreed and added that it was not only slanderous but also rude! But the first countered by saying, "I never said anything about a person that would make me look back to see if that person were standing behind me."

Imagine being so good that you never had to worry if anyone was listening. *That's* ethical leadership!

Jewish Bright Spot

Rabbi Israel Meir Kagan (1838–1933) became known as the Chofetz Chaim, meaning "eager for life," after the title of his well-known book on the laws relating to speech, which was in turn named from Psalms (34:13–14): "Who is the person that desires life, who desires years of good fortune? Guard your tongue from evil, your lips from deceitful speech."

1. What do you see as the connection between being eager for life and guarding what you say?

2. Why would refraining from gossip give you years of good fortune?

3. What's one small way you can "guard your tongue" and keep yourself from gossiping?

21

Say What You Mean, Mean What You Say

When you have to speak in front of others, do you . . .

- Blush?

- Feel weak in the knees?

- Sweat profusely?

- Fear you'll forget what to say?

- Rush through speaking to get it over with?

- Stumble?

- Doubt anyone's listening?

- Hold notes in front of your face so you can disappear?

Comedian Jerry Seinfeld talks about a study showing that public speaking was the number one fear of the average person, with number two being death. "This means," he says, "that to the average person, if you have to be at a funeral, you'd rather be in the casket than doing the eulogy."

In the Torah, Moses didn't think he was a gifted speaker; in fact, he had the chutzpah to tell God that he wasn't the man for the job because of it: "I have never been a man of words, either in times past or now that You have spoken to Your servant; I am slow of speech and slow of tongue." (Exodus 4:10) Moses feared that no one would take him seriously: "What if they do not believe me and do not listen to me?" (Exodus 4:1) It sounds like Moses had the same kind of stage fright that terrorizes so many of us.

- How often do you speak in front of a group?

- What emotions do you feel when thinking of speaking publicly? Excitement? Anxiety? Nervousness?

- As we just read, Moses struggled with self-confidence and self-esteem. If you experience any of these struggles, do they get in the way of your leadership?

Effective communication skills are essential for leadership. Sure, you're also communicating when you write high-impact emails, texts, and meaningful thank-you notes, more on that later, but if you're going to lead, you're likely to be in front of a group sometimes. It may sound scary, but it can also be fun.

Estee Portnoy is the business manager and spokesperson for the NBA Hall of Famer Michael Jordan. And how did she get her start? As a teen leader in a Jewish organization, of course!

By age fifteen, as part of her local youth movement, Portnoy was planning conferences for two hundred people. "Adults advised us," Portnoy told us, "but we made a lot of decisions. We thought it was fun, but by the time I was eighteen, I knew how to lead." With her background as a dancer, she wasn't afraid to perform in front of others, but she wasn't naturally a speaker. She had to work hard at it. "Public speaking is about finding your voice." That means a journey of self-discovery: finding your passions and causes and then finding the language to share those passions. Just like playing basketball, public speaking requires thinking on your feet. It also takes practice.

Great public speakers have a gift:

- They make you feel like you're the only person in the room.

- It's as if they're talking directly to you.

- They share information while building a relationship with the audience.

- They create a warm and intimate atmosphere, even when they're speaking in front of thousands of people.

- They seem at ease—because they are.

- They look like they're really enjoying themselves—because they are!

Public speaking works best when speakers are true to themselves and speak from the heart.

Case Study

Daniella is an eleventh grader in a large public high school in Texas. During the rabbi's weekly discussion group for high school students, Daniella shared how shocked she'd felt getting off the school bus that morning and seeing two large swastikas etched into the glass of her school's doors. The school had held an assembly to talk about the incident, but Daniella still felt shaky. She burst into tears talking about the scene later, in the discussion group. Afterward, the rabbi took her aside and asked her if she would be willing to spend a few minutes next Shabbat speaking from the pulpit and talking about what she saw and how it made her feel.

Challenge: What advice would you give to Daniella to help her prepare?

US President Franklin D. Roosevelt is remembered as "the Great Communicator," one of the best speakers of the twentieth century, with his words reaching the nation over the radio for the first time in history. But he wasn't always a great orator; those who knew him recalled that at first, he was halting and lacked confidence. A few tricks helped him gain confidence, but he always kept his talks earnest and plain-spoken. So it makes sense that he summed up his own philosophy on public speaking in so few words: "Be sincere; be brief; be seated."

To help you gain confidence, here are some hacks we've discovered from successful speakers:

- **Watch and imitate influential speakers.** Watch video clips of terrific speakers: teachers, celebrities, athletes, scholars, or politicians (TED talks are a great place to start). Listen to the content, but also observe their body language—the way they move and pause. Take notes.

- **Start small.** Find opportunities to speak to small groups of people, such as at meetings or informal get-togethers. Forget about the stage for now. Work your way up. (A great small way to get started is also by introducing someone else—see below!)

- **Personalize your remarks.** Listeners pay the most attention to meaningful personal stories. Whatever you're going to say—even if it's facts, numbers, or instructions—try to tell a piece of your story, especially a conflict or problem you overcame. A Jewish expression says, "Words that come from the heart enter the heart."

- **Make eye contact.** Build trust by looking straight into listeners' eyes. You could even try focusing on one person per sentence. Or for a short speech, you might want to make a broader visual sweep of the room a few times.

- **Less is more.** The longer the better? Nope. Abraham Lincoln's Gettysburg address was only 271 words long and only took him about two minutes to recite. The speaker before him had spoken for two hours. Hardly anyone remembers that speech or speaker. (It was Edward Everett.)

- **Keep introductions short.** One great way to start speaking in public is by introducing someone else. But please don't stand up and read their bio. Just thank everybody for coming, say a few words about the speaker and your connection to them, and then—as Roosevelt said—"Be seated.

- **Let your body speak.** Let your body language show your enthusiasm for your topic by using your arms and hands to support your words. Stand tall and confident (even if you don't *feel* confident).

- **Breathe deeply.** Before you take the stage, drop your shoulders and breathe deeply in through your nose and then out through your mouth. This should relax your shoulders and oxygenate your chest. Shallow breathing can intensify your anxiety.

- **Know your audience.** Speaking is not about you—it's always about your audience. Figure out who they are before you speak. You should tailor the content and tone to your audience.

- **Pause dramatically.** Don't hurry through your remarks; it's not a race to the finish line. And talking too fast can be exhausting for your audience. Slow down, pause, catch your breath. Help your mind catch up to your body; you can use pauses to prepare your audience for an important thought.

- **Share one thought well.** Commit to one idea and one idea only and develop it along a clear and logical path. If you're preparing a *d'var Torah* or a short spiritual message, don't try to teach the whole Torah; stick to your one key idea and deliver it in the best way you can.

- **Start strong and end strong.** How interesting and compelling are your first and last sentences? Those are your anchors. When you start out strong, your audience wants to follow you further. End on a high note and you lift peoples' spirits.

- **Give them a mission.** You have your audience's attention. What are you going to do with it? Do you want people to give tzedakah, volunteer, protest, support an issue, build a community, make a new friend? Present a call to action now that they've been inspired.

- **Say thank you.** Sure, it's essential to express gratitude. But beginning or ending with a long list of names is guaranteed to lose your audience and perhaps offend someone you forgot to thank. Instead, list their names on the program and ask people to look at it.

- **Ditch your notes.** Nothing says "I don't care about my audience" more than reading your speech from a piece of paper. For one thing, you can't make eye contact with listeners if you're reading your speech. Try giving yourself just a few bullet points on an index card (or a few index cards).

- **They don't know what you didn't say.** Forgot something you wanted to say? Didn't get a chance to work in that joke you'd been practicing? You're the only one who knows about it. So unless what you forgot was essential, just shrug and move on. There will be a next time.

- **Practice.** Nothing beats practice. Volunteer for every speaking opportunity you can find, starting small and working your way up. As Franklin D. Roosevelt discovered, practice always pays off, and you'll pick up tips and tricks along the way that will make it even easier next time.

You've got this.

Jewish Bright Spot

Jeremiah was very young—some say only a teenager—when he became a prophet. Like Moses, Jeremiah thought he was not fit to lead. He claimed he was too young for the job: "Ah, Adonai God! I don't know how to speak, for I am still a boy." But God responded, "Do not say, 'I am still a boy,' but go wherever I send you and speak whatever I command you." (Jeremiah 1:6–7)

1. How does God convince Jeremiah to overcome his resistance?

2. Have you ever said or thought you're too young to lead? How did you overcome that thought?

3. How could you encourage others to get involved who may see themselves as too young or inexperienced?

22

WRITE IT BETTER

Anything that has your name on it is a reflection of you.

When you lead, whatever you write is also, whether you like it or not, a reflection of your organization. You may need to send out an email about an event or a fundraising campaign or a note to parents with safety protocols at a Shabbaton. Every text, email, and social media post is an expression of you that may stay in cyberspace forever. So here are a few questions to guide you in keeping your written communication as effective and professional as it can be.

- Is what I'm writing necessary?

- Is it kind?

- Is it as brief as it needs to be?

- Could it possibly be misinterpreted?

Because it's so easy to communicate in writing, we don't always think twice. But when we lead, our words carry extra weight. In Hebrew, the word *d'var* can mean "word," as in a *d'var Torah* (a "word of Torah"), but it also means "thing." Our words, just like physical things, have weight and impact. Treat your own words seriously because when you're a leader, others will as well.

Inner Workout

- What kind of writing do you need to do as part of your leadership role(s)?

- Name something you have written that you wish you could take back.

Because your words can have weight and impact, it's important to think about how you write for different audiences. Spelling mistakes are fine in a text to a friend but not in an email request to your neighbor to sponsor your bike ride for charity. Either way, it can help to look everything over one more time before sending. Even a text to a friend might benefit from one more quick look to make sure it can't be misunderstood.

Try these pro tips when representing your cause or organization in writing:

- For every piece of writing—text, email, or otherwise—read through to the end before sending. Consider having someone else look it over as well.

- Watch out for the basics: double-check spelling, grammar, and capital letters, and use emojis sparingly.

- Less is more.

- Make sure your header or subject line is clear.

- Make sure there is no text after your message that you *don't* want included.

Remember that not everything you think belongs in writing. If what you've written is sensitive or could be taken the wrong way, consider waiting an hour or even a day before sending it. And before you press send, ask yourself: "Who is the person I'd least like to read this?" That can help you decide whether you need to make changes to your message before you send it so it will reflect well on you and your organization.

At Mount Sinai, the Jewish people received the Ten Commandments both orally and in writing: "Then Moses turned and went down from the mountain with the two tablets of the testimony in his hand, tablets which were written on both sides; they were written on one side and the other. The tablets were God's work, and the writing was God's writing engraved on the tablets." (Exodus 32:15–16)

1. Why was it important to write down these words?

2. What do you gain spiritually from writing that you may not from speaking? What is the benefit to the reader?

3. If you could chisel any words in stone—a rule or motto to live by—what would they be?

23

CONTROL YOUR NEED TO CONTROL

If you're a leader, chances are that someone—a friend, parent, or sibling—has called you "bossy" or something similar: strong-willed, domineering, pushy. But you may see yourself simply as someone who gets the job done. We need bossy leaders sometimes, but let's face it: no one likes to be bossed around.

When the debate team that Judah started with some of his friends grew from four people to forty, they started complaining that he was being mean or bossy. When they wouldn't buckle down, he told us, "I closed their laptops and said it was time to work, but maybe that wasn't a good way to motivate them to win. I should have been more positive instead of seeming like the grouch."

Besides his local youth movement, Judah was already leading several activities: organizing marathons, helping run his synagogue youth minyan, running the Mock Trial team and Model UN at his school, along with an Israel Action Club. So he was a natural to help run the debate team. But his leadership style was starting to alienate some people he cared about, forcing him to rethink the way he led the team:

> When we started, it was informal. Just a few of us. I could talk to my friends, and it wasn't hard to figure things out logistically. As it grew bigger, I needed to keep people engaged and prepared and have the knowledge to do well on a large scale because I couldn't work personally with everyone. I had to lay down some infrastructure to support the team.

Like most people, Judah doesn't like to be told what to do. Yet in this situation, he found himself turning around and doing it to others. And they did not like it.

- Describe a "bossy" moment you have experienced.

- Who has bossed you around?

- Describe what it felt like.

In the Torah, Moses's father-in-law, Yitro, saw the long lines of people waiting to ask questions of Moses, and he confronted him bluntly: "What is this thing that you are doing to the people? Why do you act alone, while all the people stand about you from morning until evening?" (Exodus 18:14) Yitro advised Moses to delegate responsibility. Moses listened and divided up the work as Yitro suggested, saving both himself and the people from exhaustion.

From Yitro's intervention in this one small episode you can find a few tips for managing your inner boss:

- Be open to advice.

- Don't micromanage.

- Delegate authority.

- Trust that if you give someone else a job, they'll do it. Send gentle reminders if they don't.

- Praise and thank people often so that leading feels like an enjoyable team effort.

Having authority is not the same thing as having influence, as Judah learned the hard way. When you have influence, you can persuade others by virtue of your ideas, charisma, and commitment, and you don't need to boss anyone around—which is better for those you lead and for you as well. Over time, Judah figured that out and developed ways for the debate team to work together more collaboratively without compromising on the fun.

Jewish Bright Spot

Joshua, who has a whole biblical book named after him, had to rise to the challenge of leadership. He was young; Moses just died. The Israelites were on the brink of entering the Promised Land. They needed a brave, strong leader who could carry on Moses's vision while also forging his own identity. Joshua had to help the Israelites transition to his leadership after forty years of following Moses. But even in the very first chapter of the book of Joshua, the Israelites express their strong support: "We will do everything you have commanded us, and we will go wherever you send us. We will obey you just as we obeyed Moses. . . . Only be strong and of good courage!" (Joshua 1:16–17)

1. Why did the people say this to Joshua—and why in this specific way?

2. Why did Joshua need to hear this message at the very moment he took over from Moses?

3. When did you take on a leadership role that required extra strength and courage?

Thanks for the Feedback

24

Jack, sixteen, was having a tough time as the captain of his soccer team. One player kept hogging the ball, clearly thinking he was the best player. "Someone was always mad," Jack told us.

Jack had other leadership roles in school and outside of it, and they were all going pretty well. But soccer was a hassle every single day.

He started getting stomachaches right before practice. "We weren't having a great season, and we had a lot of pushback from the kids for losing so many games. Soccer just wasn't fun anymore." Jack knew he had to do something about all the fighting on the team or it was going to ruin their entire season. So he sat down with the player who'd been hogging the ball:

> I said, "Something has to change. I understand you want a bigger role, but the way you're doing it is not effective and not helping the team. No one is going to enjoy the season. You've got to stop. This isn't helping anyone."

Without knowing it, Jack was observing an important mitzvah: not bearing a grudge. As the Torah says, "You should surely correct your friend." (Leviticus 19:17) This is part of a cluster of laws about how to treat other people, including correcting someone who is misbehaving. When we don't speak up, we can develop increasingly negative feelings, which we keep bottled up. Instead of sharing our true feelings, we may pull away, never giving that person the chance to make amends.

As Jack learned, it isn't easy to speak up. But in his case, it actually worked. It helped that Jack didn't only speak to the teammate who was hogging the ball. He also asked the other team members to work with the player during practice to build a lighter and more pleasant atmosphere. Over time, his teammate grew into his role, because Jack made space for everyone to be heard and had the courage to share feedback productively. The team didn't win every game, but they salvaged the season, and they all matured as a result. Jack's team admired the thoughtful way he'd handled the situation, and this helped him become a more effective and respected leader.

Inner Workout

- Think of some feedback you received from a parent or teacher. Write it down and the impact it had on you.

- Now think of feedback you received from someone your own age. How was it different? How did you respond?

- Do you have feedback for someone? What's holding you back from giving it?

Giving feedback is hard work, and it doesn't always achieve the results we hope for. Receiving feedback isn't easy either. In Proverbs (9:8), we learn that if we correct a thoughtful person, they'll love us, but if we correct a fool, they'll hate us. Feedback helps us grow, but that doesn't always make it any easier to hear. In fact, Jack believes being able to receive feedback is an even more import-ant leadership skill than being able to give it:

> You have to be able to take constructive criticism. Ninety-nine percent of teen leadership roles will involve other people. You never get to decide by yourself what you're doing. The tension builds up, and it's never discussed until you get to the breaking point. I welcome the feedback. You can nod your head and make no effort to change, but then people don't want to work with you.

When problems arise, try to listen with an open heart and mind, or the issues can get worse—to the point where they seem insurmountable. Here are a few suggestions for listening receptively when someone is giving you feedback:

- Check in for clarity by repeating what you've heard. (We mentioned something similar in chapter 18 about active listening.)

- Try not to be defensive. It gets in the way of really hearing.

- Assume good intent. Most of the time, people genuinely want to help you improve.

It's hard to hear negative feedback, but it's also hard to give it. When you find yourself in the position of having to give somebody feedback, here are a few ways you can make sure your message gets through:

- Write down what you want to say ahead of time to help formulate your thoughts clearly.

- Focus on only one issue, even if there is more than one issue you'd like to address. That makes it easier for the other person to hear and respond positively.

- Include the benefits or possible outcomes of following the feedback.

- Deliver your feedback privately and kindly while reassuring the person that they are valued.

Jewish Bright Spot

In his "Laws of Human Character," Maimonides writes that when a person needs to give feedback, "It is essential that the criticism be shared privately. They should speak calmly. Employ soft language, and explain that the criticism is being shared only for their own good."

1. Why is privacy and calm important?

2. Why would anyone give feedback that was not for the other person's good?

3. Think of a time you have given or received feedback. How did calm and privacy (or the lack thereof) affect the process?

WORKING WITH ADULTS

Working with parents and other supportive adults who encourage your independence and growth can help you save time, work more effectively, minimize drama, and benefit from collaboration. Oversight, involvement, and direction from adults can help you grow your leadership platform. At the same time, it can introduce challenges, including everyday annoyances and miscommunications that can get in the way of what you need to accomplish.

One of the most powerful mentor relationships described in the Bible is the one between the prophet Elijah (who, according to Jewish tradition, "visits" every Passover seder and circumcision) and his disciple Elisha. Elisha was a young farmer working in the family's fields when Elijah sought him out and literally threw his mantle of leadership on him. Elisha kissed his mother and father goodbye, then left on an amazing leadership adventure. This relationship gave each of them something essential: Elijah couldn't carry the challenges of leadership alone, while Elisha needed mentoring and wisdom to grow into the kind of leader who could one day step into Elijah's shoes.

The best adult mentors let younger leaders make their own mistakes without swooping in to give advice or judgment while creating space for them to reflect on their leadership challenges when *they* are ready. These adults—parents, counselors, teachers, youth movement professionals—often become mentors and friends for life.

Here's what some teen leaders have said about the adults who support their work and what they can do to set better expectations in these working relationships:

"The best adults for teens to work with are empathic and good problem-solvers."
    —Jacklyn

"If the person in charge believes in me, I have more confidence, and it helps me feel that I belong where I am. That's also true for being appreciated."
    —David

"Some adults helped us be realistic about safety and helped us figure out what's financially reasonable."
    —Jake

"The ideal authority figure for me to work with is someone who helps with logistics and takes on some of the jobs that aren't fun, that are often placed on teens unnecessarily."
    —Noa

"I think it's been helpful to have an adult figure present, around and available, a go-to person who also steps back to let kids have the space to experiment and learn from our mistakes but not drown in them."
    —Melissa

"Teens should never go rogue. As a teenager, you think you're invincible and no one can touch you. But it's not true. You need adults to help you at the beginning, middle, and end. But if there are too many adults, it stops being a program or event for teens."
    —Daniel

- Describe, in one paragraph, an important mentor for you. Include ways in which they've helped you and character traits you admire.

- Name adults you work with in your leadership roles. How's it going?

- What do you think adults can gain by working closely with you?

- When is the last time you complimented or thanked an adult who mentors you?

Adult mentoring can be very helpful. But when adults are too controlling, overbearing, or temperamental, young leaders can feel under-supported and unhappy.

> "I've gotten yelled at or glared at by adults. Sometimes adults yell at kids in leadership roles, but they wouldn't do that to fellow adults."
> —Daniel

> "When I got negative feedback, and I was tired, I checked out."
> —Melissa

> "I find it difficult working with authority figures who don't understand how teens operate or what they like to do. We were shut down a lot."
> —Jacklyn

> "You need adult supervision but in so, so many of these cases, the adults need supervising."
> —Ilana

> "It doesn't matter how old you are, you can have an opinion. We don't have the same authority as adults but we are equals in terms of the respect we deserve as human beings."
> —Julia

Some of these problems can be avoided with good, open communication. Let the adults you're working with know what's working and what's not working so that the relationship can be truly helpful and enriching to both of you.

But sometimes these relationships simply don't work out due to personality clashes or different work styles. Problems can also arise when roles are not clearly defined. "Advisors or youth directors can have a really hard time creating boundaries," warns Alexis, a college student who had negative experiences with several adults as a teen leader. Adults may misunderstand what responsibilities are realistic for a young leader or fail to respect their other commitments. They may come across as condescending or overly demanding when they are just trying to be helpful.

Setting boundaries is about not only limiting and clarifying your workload but also about the relationship itself. For example, Alexis says advisors sometimes pick favorites. "They're close and get a lot of work done together. They text and Facetime, which is lovely for those kids who feel great about themselves, but sad for other kids who don't get that attention." She adds, "And that kind of closeness makes it harder when the advisor needs to put their foot down."

When the boundaries between a working relationship and friendship blur, it can make the relationship unproductive and lead to inappropriate interactions. As Alexis told us, "Sometimes my youth work felt unprofessional. But the more professional it was, the more impact it had on me." For Alexis, "unprofessional" referred to adults who did not do what they said they would, did not follow up, told inappropriate jokes, or bossed teens around simply because they thought they could.

Inner Workout

- Have you ever experienced a teen/adult relationship firsthand where boundaries were not set?

- What did you do about it?

- Could you have handled it differently or better?

Although it's rare, if adults don't establish appropriate boundaries, they may take advantage of the power balance to flirt with teens or exploit their vulnerabilities. They may be manipulative about task assignments and punitive when those tasks don't get done. That's why teen leaders and other adults need to be vigilant in spotting warning signs—using inappropriate language; asking to be alone in a space; or texting, emailing, or calling at odd hours—and reporting them to responsible adults.

Teen leaders must protect not only themselves but also other teens who may find themselves in potentially inappropriate or abusive situations. That means keeping your eyes and ears open for anything that seems a little off with other teens or the general environment.

Case Study

In her final year of high school, Sophie beat the odds and got into a very exclusive internship at her local newspaper. She knows it will look great on her résumé when she applies to journalism school. Twice a week, dressed for business, Sophie goes to the newspaper office where she reports to a senior editor. He's given her a lot of meaningful responsibilities for an intern: reading submissions, editing photos, crafting social media posts, and organizing his files. Sophie notices that sometimes the senior editor is a little too friendly when she is in his office. But she's not sure. Maybe she's reading too much into his jokes or misreading innocent comments as innuendo? He seems totally normal when he's interacting with other staff. This is week two of an eight-week internship.

Challenge: What advice would you give to Sophie?

Rabbi Micah Greenland, the international director of NCSY (National Conference of Synagogue Youth), believes in training advisors to recognize emotional, physical, and sexual boundaries:

> When a person feels that at any time someone can encroach on their emotional, physical, or sexual space, they feel uncomfortable. Emotional boundaries can be less clear: how do you build a relationship that is growth-oriented but not manipulative or coercive?

Rabbi Greenland says adults who work with teens must be careful not to use love as a reward or withhold it as a punishment. And while there may be gray areas when people are working closely together, some things must be clearly and specifically off-limits:

> We have a code of conduct that is on every page of our website. We have an ombudsman and a hotline that's answered twice a day. All of that creates an environment where we not only talk the talk but walk the walk. Our guidelines aren't just recommendations. We're going to enforce them.

If you're ever unsure if something an adult has said or done is okay or inappropriate, bring someone else into the conversation. Sometimes additional guardrails are necessary to ensure that everyone feels protected. "All our youth organizations need to be safe havens," says Rabbi Greenland.

Establishing secure boundaries with adults to keep relationships helpful and constructive is essential for creating that kind of safe haven. In the next chapter we'll explore ways that teens can set boundaries among themselves as a further step toward building healthy leadership communities.

Jewish Bright Spot

Along with the rest of the Ten Commandments, the Torah tells us twice to honor our parents:

- "Honor your father and your mother, that you may long endure on the land that Adonai your God is assigning to you." (Exodus 20:12)

- "Honor your father and your mother, as Adonai your God has commanded you, that you may long endure, and that you may fare well, in the land that Adonai your God is assigning to you." (Deuteronomy 5:16)

1. What are the differences between these verses and why would honoring parents help people live long on the land?

2. What are some of the challenges involved in honoring parents?

3. How can honoring parents translate into building working relationships with other adults?

26

CREATING SACRED COMMUNITIES

In the previous chapter, we saw how establishing clear boundaries between adult mentors and teen leaders can help create safe, healthy working relationships. There's another boundary we also need to discuss: saying no to hookup culture when teens get together.

Not long ago, six brave older teens from many different youth groups cowrote an essay, "For Continuity's Sake? Addressing Hookup Culture in Jewish Youth Groups," criticizing the hypersexualization of Jewish teen events. They felt that some teen events can unintentionally promote misogyny and build unhealthy relationships devoid of intimacy and respect. The writers pointed to intense peer pressure to engage in sexualized activity, like a points system to "grade" other teens, typically females.

Don't be afraid to say no to the kind of behavior that belittles your physical dignity and demeans your body and soul. Give yourself permission to set those boundaries for yourself. No one else can advocate for you the way you can.

In an earlier chapter, we talked about saying no to leadership responsibilities that don't speak to you. There's another no that is important: saying no to being involved in anything that's not 100 percent consensual. Or anything you're not comfortable doing. This might take courage in the face of peer pressure, but it will protect your privacy and ultimately bring you and your body the respect you deserve. So before you say yes, ask yourself these questions:

- Will I regret this tomorrow, next month, next year?

- Is this what I want for myself?

- Does the person asking or expecting something from me actually care about me?

- Will getting involved with this person complicate my life or other relationships I value?

A kind no can help preserve friendships and maintain a healthy dynamic within your organization.

In leadership, this doesn't only mean trying to act as a role model; it also means establishing an atmosphere of safety and sexual security at every single program or event you're part of. Some factors that contribute to a sexualized environment include misogynistic or sexualized music, program choices that encourage rather than inhibit certain behaviors, and physical spaces that are not open enough to make sure organizers can monitor the safety of all participants.

Jewish Bright Spot

Setting boundaries is important in life—and also in Jewish law. The Torah says, "You shall not move your neighbor's boundary mark, set up by previous generations, in the property that will be allotted to you in the land that Adonai your God is giving you to possess." (Deuteronomy 19:14)

1. What is the principle behind this law?

2. Describe a relationship in your life where the boundaries are fuzzy and need to be clarified.

3. How might you apply this general ruling to setting safe boundaries for others?

How to Have That Difficult Conversation

In chapter 24, we talked about effective ways of giving and receiving feedback. But sometimes leadership demands more—such as a really difficult conversation. Many teens we interviewed told us that tough conversations are one of the hardest challenges they face and that sometimes it's easier to have a difficult conversation with an adult, like a parent or teacher, than with a friend. How do you tell a teammate that they've hurt you or someone else? How do you tell a friend that they have a drinking problem or that they need to stop the drama or own up to a big mistake? These are high-stakes conversations that require extra sensitivity.

Can you think of three difficult conversations you need to have but probably won't?

1. _____

2. _____

3. _____

It's downright impossible to lead without having some difficult conversations. Whenever you're working with people, chances are you'll have to make someone uncomfortable at some point. It's even harder when you're friends with that person, or if they might resent being told what to do by someone their own age.

● What makes a conversation difficult for you?

● Recall a difficult conversation and what happened as a result. Jot down some memories of it.

● Think of a difficult conversation you need to have. What's holding you back? What would make it easier?

Susan Scott, a veteran executive coach and business speaker, has been "challenging people to say the things that are hard to say" for over two decades. She believes in the power of honesty and in getting to the point quickly. If you have something difficult to say, Scott warns, don't ask the other person how they're doing or engage in small talk.

Scott also doesn't love the popular "Oreo cookie" or "compliment sandwich" method of introducing a tough topic, where you start with a compliment, then give criticism, and then wrap things up with another compliment. Some people only hear the compliments; others only hear the criticism. And beyond this, she says, the next time you offer a compliment, they won't trust you.

One final piece of advice from Scott: avoid being a "Machine Gun Nelly." This is a person who's so scared of tough conversations that once they get the other person's attention, they spew everything that's wrong, then duck and run away. This is disrespectful, not to mention overwhelming to the other person. Choosing one issue to focus on will help them understand what's really wrong.

When you need to have a difficult conversation, you will probably achieve a better outcome if you plan ahead for a dialogue that is respectful, inviting, clear, and focused on your goals. Scott uses a helpful seven-step formula for "better" difficult conversations. Following a formula doesn't mean the conversation has to be scripted; it just takes away some of the emotional sting and helps you prepare so that you come across as well as possible.

Seven Steps to a Better Difficult Conversation

1. Name the issue.

2. Select a specific example that illustrates the behavior you want to change.

3. Describe your emotions about the issue.

4. Clarify what is at stake.

5. Identify your contribution to the problem.

6. Indicate the wish to resolve the issue.

7. Invite the other person to respond.

Let's use a simple example to show how these steps might look. Jason, your co-captain on the volleyball team, has been late for every practice over the last month. The coach is new and not comfortable having that conversation, so it's up to you to speak to Jason. Here's what your plan for that conversation might look like:

1. **Name the issue:** "Jason, thanks for making time to talk today. I want to talk about how you've been coming late to practice this past month."

2. **Offer specific examples:** "Last Sunday, Monday, and Thursday, you showed up a half hour late."

3. **Describe your emotions:** "I feel frustrated about this because we're supposed to be in this together, and the team expects us to be role models."

4. **Clarify what's at stake:** "If we don't take this seriously, everyone else will start coming late, too."

5. **Identify your contribution:** "I really should have talked to you about this after the first few times. So you may not have realized how important it is to be on time."

6. **Indicate your wish to resolve the issue:** "I really want to resolve this and have a great season. You're a great player and an asset to the team."

7. **Invite the other person to respond:** "I'd love to hear your thoughts and learn what I can do to help."

By naming the problem respectfully instead of beating around the bush, and by offering examples, you are leading well and trying to identify a problem clearly. In this example, Jason now knows how this is impacting you emotionally and what the stakes are for the team.

You also need to own your contribution to the problem—and you *do* contribute to the problem, always. Maybe you waited too long to tell this person how the behavior impacts you and others. Maybe you haven't stressed teamwork enough. By showing your desire to resolve the problem, you are letting
Jason know that you value him and want to see him succeed. And by concluding with an invitation to respond, you've let him know that his voice on this issue is important, too, and that it will be heard.

Growing up in Auckland, New Zealand, Noah had never stepped into a synagogue, fasted on Yom Kippur, or had a family seder at Passover. But in his final year of high school, he began dating Ilana, who invited Noah for Friday-night Shabbat dinner at her home. He loved it. Over time, Noah started joining Ilana's family at synagogue and participating in her youth movement. He's trying to learn more about Judaism and avoiding bacon and seafood at family meals. But when Noah tries to talk to his parents about his spiritual growth, they shrug it off as a phase, implying that when Noah breaks up with Ilana, he'll break up with Judaism, too. Noah has always been close with his parents and wants them to take his journey more seriously.

Challenge: What advice would you give to Noah? (Feel free to use our seven-step conversation to help him plan his response.)

Practice Makes Perfect

Outline a difficult conversation you need to have with a friend, parent, or sibling following the seven steps we've explored in this chapter:

1. Name the issue.

2. Select a specific example that illustrates the behavior you want to change.

3. Describe your emotions about this issue.

4. Clarify what is at stake.

5. Identify your contribution to the problem.

6. Indicate your wish to resolve the issue.

7. Invite your partner to respond.

The first few times you have a difficult conversation, it can be daunting. But gaining practice, being patient with the process, and, most importantly, seeing positive results can encourage you to keep having these conversations when needed. Tough conversations are hard but when done well, gentle honesty can actually strengthen a relationship and eliminate the resentment that builds when our own needs are ignored or not noticed. Don't take our word for it; try it yourself.

Jewish Bright Spot

Good leadership involves knowing when a tough conversation will be effective and when to stay quiet because talking about a problem might make it worse or could sour the relationship. As the Talmud states, "Your silence is preferable to your speech."

1. What do you think this means?

2. When has your silence been preferable to your speech in your leadership?

3. When did you take the risk and your speech was preferable to your silence?

Fundraising and Friend-Raising

Looking back on her time in high school, Michal, who's now twenty, estimates that she probably raised over $10,000 for tzedakah. She got started fundraising in fifth grade for Hoops for Heart, probably more for the prizes than anything else, but by ninth grade, she was raising money and awareness for the causes that truly moved her and building community and friendships as a result. "I don't feel awkward asking for money," Michal says now, "because I'm confident I'm raising for important things, and I only ask from people who I know have the capacity to give."

As the Talmud says, "Doing the right thing for the wrong reason can lead to doing the right thing for the right reason." Like Michal, you've probably sold *something*—chocolates, wrapping paper, T-shirts—at some point to raise money for a sports team, student council, or charitable organization. Or maybe you've participated in a bake sale, car wash, carnival, or half-marathon to raise money. But if someone were to ask you, "Do you *like* raising money?" you'd probably say no.

It would be easier if every time you asked for money, everyone would give what they could. But we usually assume the answer will be no, and no one likes to be rejected. So we often don't bother asking in the first place. But Michal's not worried: "Most people don't reject kids." Even though that's not everyone's experience, getting used to hearing no and managing rejection is an important leadership lesson, and it can help teach resilience.

When things go right and you get one yes after another, it feels magical; that's part of what got Michal hooked. "Starting at a young age, I understood the importance of tzedakah and raising money for things you care about. You have to learn skills to ask others to help people in need."

Michal learned those skills as a member of a Jewish organization that trains teens to raise and allocate funds. It taught her how to advocate for causes she believes in. You may have a similar organization in your community. (Try asking your local Jewish Federation or another community organization.)

Inner Workout

- When you have money to give, what causes matter most to you?

- If you have raised money, how much was it, what was the cause, and how did your donation make you feel about the organization?

- How do you feel, emotionally and physically, at the thought of asking for money?

Not everyone has Michal's bubbly approach and fearlessness. The very thought of asking someone for money might make you tense up, start sweating, or feel sick or even nauseated. What if you don't do a great job explaining or promoting your cause and they say no or slam the door in your face? Oy.

But wait a minute—what is money for if not to ease others' suffering? Judaism expects everybody, even the poor, to give part of their income to charity. Can you imagine a world where everyone did that? We could eradicate poverty and hunger. When you focus on the end goal and not the "ask," it can empower you. Because you actually *can* do something to help eradicate poverty, end hunger, or contribute in a thousand other ways to making the world better through tzedakah. Every time you inspire someone to say yes, that gift can be traced back to *you*. It would never have happened without you.

This exercise will help you focus on that end goal—making a difference in the world through a cause you care about.

Making a Perfect Pitch

Think of an organization you care about. Write two clear and compelling sentences about what it does, to help interest others:

1.

2.

Write two sentences about why it's important to you personally:

1.

2.

Write your emotions about the cause:

1.

2.

Write your "ask" in one sentence:

From all her fundraising activities, Michal also learned other skills. She learned how and when to make the ask, how to write a good email and thank-you note, and how to prioritize her own giving of tzedakah with the money she has made working so that it matches what she cares about most. Other important leadership skills that teens can learn from fundraising include being an ambassador for an organization, talking to adults, developing self-esteem, budgeting, and handling money responsibly.

Case Study

Jesse, fifteen, lost his favorite aunt two years ago to breast cancer. He's been giving small amounts, but he knows he could do more if he got others to give as well. So when he heard about a hundred-mile bike ride to support breast cancer research, he immediately set up a page to raise the $3,600 he needed to participate. He posted the page on social media and emailed the link to some close relatives and friends with the sign-off, "No pressure." But Jesse *does* feel pressure to raise the money; he really wants to participate but so far has only raised $1,000, mostly from his parents and an uncle.

Challenge: What advice would you give to Jesse?

In the next chapter, we'll explore some helpful techniques for fundraising. Remember that every time you ask for money for a good cause, you are giving others a mitzvah moment; you're actually doing them a favor. And although we translate the Hebrew word *tzedakah* as "charity," it actually comes from a root word meaning "justice." Tzedakah helps us create a more just, fair, and compassionate world. Thank you for giving and getting others to give!

Jewish Bright Spot

The Torah suggests that if we live charitably, there will be no poverty: "There shall be no needy among you—since Adonai your God will bless you in the land." (Deuteronomy 15:4) But only a few verses later, it offers advice for helping those in need: "If, however, there is a needy person among you . . . do not harden your heart and shut your hand against your needy kinsman. Rather, you must open your hand and lend him whatever he needs." (Deuteronomy 15:7–8)

1. How do you understand this contradiction?

2. What kind of ideal society are these verses describing? Do you think this is possible?

3. Why do we harden our hearts in front of those who are needy?

29

Eight Fundraising Hacks

Almost ready to get out there and inspire others to give? In the previous chapter, we talked about the power and importance of fundraising. Now it's time to get started. Here are eight fundraising hacks to prepare you for the sacred work ahead.

1. Make a list of potential donors.

You know more people than you think. Write down all the people you know. Don't stop yourself by imagining why each might *not* give you a donation. Let them make that decision. Imagine that they'd *love* to give you a donation. Write down family members first, then your friends, adult family friends, teachers, youth leaders, and others in your community.

2. Create an inspiring pitch.

Create a picture in your mind of one person who would benefit from their donation, actually visualizing how they would benefit. Now include that picture in your pitch. Provide one sentence about the organization and then tell them the amount you'd like them to contribute. (Hint: don't tell them how much you hate fundraising; tell them how much you love the cause!) Before your first ask, share your pitch with someone who can give you honest and helpful feedback. Ask them:

- Did I stay on point?

- Was my pitch too long or too short?

- Did I personalize the message to the person listening?

- Did my written pitch (such as an email or social media post) have any typos or mistakes?

3. Set realistic expectations.

Consult with others to decide how much is reasonable to ask individuals for. If your expectations are too high, you'll be disappointed, and you may give up altogether. If you have lower expectations, you'll be pleasantly surprised when you hit your target and exceed it.

4. Practice, practice, practice.

For every photograph that makes it into a newspaper or magazine, the photographer may have taken dozens or even hundreds of photos that will never be published. The hockey Hall of Famer Wayne Gretzky said, "You miss one hundred percent of the shots you don't take." It's also true for raising money. Look at every no as a dress rehearsal for your next yes.

5. Make it personal.

Explain what this cause means to you personally and why you got involved. Anyone can read on a website what a charity does. What you need to share is your personal connection. Be careful not to put down other organizations or causes, but make it clear why you chose *this* one instead of all the others out there. That makes all the difference.

6. Ask first, follow up later.

Sometimes people forget to respond, especially to emails. We all need gentle reminders (but not too many; sometimes we need to also take the hint). When someone gives, thank them right away and then again in writing (handwritten notes send a classy message of gratitude). Fundraising research suggests that people need to be thanked right away and seven times in total for them to feel appreciated. Expressing gratitude builds the relationship, which will help the next time you ask them to donate.

7. Be thankful even for a no.

There are many reasons people say no. It may be a bad time. They may be having financial difficulties or have already given to other causes. When we are gracious even when they say no, we leave the door open to ask them again at a time when they are in a better position to donate. More importantly, it's the right thing to do.

8. Don't gossip (even if they don't give).

Fundraising can create opportunities for lashon hara, speaking badly about those you ask for money—whether or not they give. It might be tempting to say something like, "They're driving that expensive car but they can only give me a check for thirty-six dollars?" or "Who does she think she is? I gave her twice as much last year when she asked me." Rather than judging, just thank them, respect their decision, and keep it private. After all, that's how you'd like to be treated.

Feel readier now?

Get ready. Get set. *Go.*

Jewish Bright Spot

In one of the more well-known teachings in Pirkei Avot (Ethics of the Fathers), Rabbi Tarfon says, "It is not your duty to finish the task, but neither are you at liberty to neglect it." (2:16)

1. When fundraising, we can always do a little bit more, so how do you decide how much is enough?

2. How do you balance the two elements of what Rabbi Tarfon is saying?

3. When is it time to pass on your fundraising role to someone else to take over?

30

AN ATTITUDE OF GRATITUDE

Gratitude might not change everything, but it can make us feel a lot better about ourselves, others, and the situations we find ourselves in. In the Jewish tradition, the first words spoken in the morning are "*Modeh ani*," which express gratitude to God for returning our soul. We are alive for another day, so let's make it the best possible day. In fact, the Hebrew word for Jew, *Yehudi*, comes from the same Hebrew root, meaning "thanks."

But after we wake up and the day starts, life can get very busy very quickly. We are pulled in many different directions. When leading isn't easy, we may start feeling depleted. We forget the Modeh Ani of the morning. Leadership can involve many thankless moments; times when we feel overworked and underappreciated. We may want recognition and validation for our efforts and find that no one is paying attention. Or worse: people complain!

The best way to get thanks is to give thanks. Research tells us that being grateful every day is good for our health. It's also good for our leadership. Everybody wants to be appreciated, so when you make others feel seen and heard, they will be more willing to partner with you. The more you thank people, the more they will want to follow your leadership.

So let's make a short gratitude list together and see how we feel.

My Gratitude List

Write ten nonobvious things you're grateful for:

1. _____

2. _____

3. _____

4. _____

5. _____

6. _____

7. _____

8. _____

9. _____

10. _____

For many families, the highlight of the Passover seder is the song "Dayeinu," which means "It would have been enough." We are grateful for every part of our Jewish story. We tell God that even if each miracle had happened alone, it would have been enough for us. Instead, we experienced miracle after miracle, and the impact of all these wonders inspires us to count our blessings. The song "Dayeinu" lists every miracle in its specific details, and that's what works best when thanking people as well. Sharing the words "thank you" alone may feel more generic, but throw in a few personal details and the message is deeper and more credible: "I really appreciated when you . . ."

● What's the best "thank you" you've ever gotten?

● What's the best "thank you" you've ever given?

Now's the moment. Write a thank-you note in your leadership capacity to someone who isn't expecting to hear from you. It doesn't have to be more than three sentences long but it *does* have to be so specific that you couldn't give it to anybody else. Here are a few prompts to help you out:

● I really noticed when you . . .

● I appreciated that you . . .

● I learned from you that . . .

Dear

With Gratitude,

Jewish tradition supplies us with a wealth of blessing texts—including blessings for receiving bad news! According to a teaching from the Talmud, "For rain and other good tidings, one recites the blessing: 'Blessed . . . Who is good and Who does good.' For bad tidings, one recites the blessing: 'Blessed . . . the true Judge.'"

1. What's one piece of good news you'd like to make a blessing on? What would the blessing say?

2. Why does the Talmud also instruct us to make blessings on bad news?

3. Think of a difficult experience you've been through that you resented at the time but are now grateful for. Write an imaginary thank-you note to the experience.

LEADING IN COMMUNITY

If not now, when?

וְאִם לֹא עַכְשָׁיו, אֵימָתַי?

V'im lo 'akhshav, eimatai?

(Pirkei Avot 1:14)

IT'S NOW

In part I of this book, we worked on self-development, the ways we can actualize ourselves so that we can lead better. In part II, we explored how leaders cope and the skills that help us lead others. In part III, we'll see how to put all these understandings and competencies to work in the real world to motivate us to innovate and inspire while we work on concrete issues facing the Jewish community and the world today.

We opened this section with the Talmudic sage Hillel's third question: "If not now, when?" If we are aware of problems right now, what are we waiting for to get started on the work of leadership? If you're like most teen leaders, you already know the answer: You don't need to wait. You can start changing the world right now.

List five burning problems you wish you could solve right now:

1. _____

_____

2. _____

_____

3. _____

_____

4. _____

_____

5. _____

- Describe one problem you applied your talents to where your efforts had a meaningful impact.

- Describe a problem you faced that was so overwhelming you wanted to give up.

- When you feel overwhelmed by the enormity of the work, what keeps you going?

According to research on how to have the most leadership impact, we need to identify problems that are large in scale, solvable, and in areas where our help is needed. These may be global or local. But it's inevitable that when we think about how difficult and pervasive problems are in the world, we may feel so small that we lose our own motivation to solve them.

When we feel overwhelmed by how much needs to be done, this reminder from Pirkei Avot (Ethics of the Fathers) 2:21 can be helpful: "You are not obligated to complete the work, but neither are you free to desist from it." One person alone probably can't solve any problem in its entirety, but that doesn't mean we can just give up. We do what we can, in the hope that someone else will continue and build upon our work, just as we are here to continue the good work of others.

One great way to get the push to get started *now* and keep going is to decide how much time you want to put toward your goal each week. Then divide up that time into measurable units each day. Let's say you want to help isolated seniors in your community. You can contact the volunteer coordinator of a senior facility, get paired with one resident, and then create a plan for visits and calls. If you have one hour a week, you might spend thirty minutes on a Sunday visit and then divide the other thirty minutes into everyday ways to reach out in five-minute increments throughout the week with texts, photos, or letters.

Another good way to encourage yourself and others to act now is by finding problems that can benefit from simple solutions. Buying one chicken or one mosquito net for a family in a developing country can have an immediate, visible, and long-lasting impact. Buying a meal for a homeless person is a goal within reach that can make a meaningful difference in one person's day.

Jewish Bright Spot

In a difficult biblical text, Sarah banished Abraham's first wife Hagar, along with Hagar's son Ishmael, to the desert. When the water ran out, Ishmael almost died of thirst. Beside herself with worry, Hagar laid him down near a bush and went to sit at a distance because she could not bear his suffering. Suddenly, at this low point in her life, she was offered a solution: "Then God opened her eyes and she saw a well of water. She went and filled the skin with water, and let the boy drink." (Genesis 21:19)

1. If the well was there the whole time, what are some possible reasons why Hagar didn't (or couldn't) see it?

2. Why do you think the Torah shared this small, heartbreaking moment with us?

3. Name a time when a solution to a problem was right in front of you but you didn't see it.

Changing the World through Tikun Olam

Romy, nineteen, spent her high school years serving on the executive committee of her school's Social Justice Club, editing its literary magazine, and coaching basketball for younger students. Her motivation to lead has been stable, consistent, and inspired by Judaism:

> *Tikun olam* is really significant to me. To me, it's about having the responsibility as a global citizen to care for others and lift others up using our voice and privilege. I always find myself asking, "What can I do to help? What is my responsibility to make this situation better?"

The phrase *tikun olam* can be translated in several ways: "to fix the world," "to repair the world," "to heal the world," or "to perfect the world." Each translation makes a different assumption about the world. In one, for instance, the world is something broken that needs fixing; in another, it is something good that can be perfected.

The concept of tikun olam appears in the Talmud and in the Aleinu, the closing prayer of most traditional services. In the second paragraph of the Aleinu, we read, "False gods will be utterly destroyed *to perfect the world* through the kingdom of God. All humankind will invoke Your name." The perfection of the world in this paragraph depends on human action in the presence of God. This aligns with the Talmud's statement that when a person dies, one of the first questions they will be asked is, "Did you hope for the world's redemption?" In other words, "Did you leave the world a better place than you found it?"

Romy has a deep desire to leave the world better than she found it. For her, that's not only about large global problems; it's also about finding many small ways to help others. "When I was a junior counselor, there was a camper who seemed really sad," she explains. "It was her first year at camp; she was feeling very homesick. So I pulled her aside, and we had a chat." The camper wanted to go home. Romy had felt exactly the same way during her first summer at camp, and she managed to convince the girl to stay just two more nights, promising they would talk again then. "The next day," Romy says, "she came running up to me and gave me a big hug. She said, 'You were right. I never want to leave!'"

Inner Workout

- What do you consider the most "broken" aspect of the world today?

- If you could fix one "broken" aspect of our world, what would it be?

- What examples from Jewish teachings and tradition—modern or biblical—have inspired you to repair the world?

When it comes to tikun olam and social justice, Hillel's first two questions, which we've used to open parts I and II of this book, sometimes seem to conflict with each other: "If I am not for myself, who will be for me? And if I am only for myself, what am I?" Understanding when to be "for yourself" and when to focus on repairing the world creates tension for all of us. When do we take care of the world? When do we take care of ourselves? If we only take care of the world, who will take care of us? But if we only take care of ourselves, how can we be a part of the larger world and expect others to be there for us?

Romy balances her desire for social justice with other aspects of Judaism that help her grow and thrive: study, character development, tzedakah to Jewish causes, and ritual observance. She is concerned that some teens devote so much time to helping the world that they neglect their own Jewish growth or forget that there are people who need help within their own communities. This is a difficult balancing act of modern Jewish life, and all leaders need to find their own way of answering these questions so they can nurture themselves and those around them while spreading goodness in the world at large.

Throughout the rest of part III, we will explore how this balancing act between repairing the world and nurturing ourselves and our own communities plays out in a number of ways: choosing leadership priorities; speaking out; and creating safe, inclusive, welcoming communities.

Jewish Bright Spot

The concept of tikun olam is also found in Kabbalah, Jewish mystical traditions and writings. In one kabbalistic account of creation, God created the world as perfect clay vessels. But in adding Divine life force into the world, the vessels shattered, scattering thousands of shards. Our job, according to this view, is to put those shards back together—to repair the world's brokenness. Each good deed is a building block of a better world, giving every act we perform truly cosmic significance. God and humans partner in the difficult work of redeeming fractures, in the spirit of the prophet Isaiah: "I Adonai, in My grace, have summoned you, and I have grasped you by the hand. I created you and appointed you a covenant people, a light of nations." (Isaiah 42:6) To do good in the world, we need to seek out places of darkness and bring our light to them.

1. How would you lead differently if you really knew that every act had cosmic significance?

2. Isaiah describes God grasping humanity "by the hand." What does this mean in terms of our mission to serve as a light of nations?

3. Describe a time you brought your light to a situation of darkness.

33

Stepping Up and Standing Up

"I love that our favorite Aussie saying is 'No worries, mate,'" says Keren from Sydney, Australia. During high school, before she started getting involved in leadership roles, Keren spent most of her time focusing on friends and grades:

> I loved tanning on Bondi Beach most days when I wasn't at school. I loved chilling with friends, watching TV, and chatting on social media. But sometimes it's good to worry. Sometimes you need to worry. Not in a bad way, but just to think how you can be more responsible.

As Keren got older, she started taking her responsibilities more seriously and challenged herself to think more broadly about what the world—and other people—needed of her. She became a counselor within her local youth movement and later, after a gap year in Israel, head *madricha* of a large Jewish day school back home in Sydney. Her world of responsibility expanded significantly, and she was proud of how meaningful her life had become because she was doing more giving.

Stepping up isn't always easy. It's hard to find the courage and space to act differently from your friends—and from how you've always acted. Looking at the Bible, we find that it wasn't always easy, even for prophets. For example, when God gave the prophet Jonah a responsibility he didn't want—to travel to Nineveh, an enemy city, and help reform it—he literally jumped on a boat sailing in the opposite direction. A storm fell at sea, but Jonah ignored it. Not only did he not step up or stand up . . . he took a nap.

Why is this story of irresponsibility included in the Bible, a book that is supposed to teach us how to live responsibly? Maybe it's because we all have "Jonah moments" when the burden of responsibility overwhelms us, and we just want to run in the opposite direction—or snooze!

God, however, did not let Jonah off so easily. Instead, God used forces of nature—a stormy sea, a large fish, a hot sun, a difficult wind, a tree, and a worm—to help Jonah rethink his desire to run away.

It's easy to think of responsibilities as someone else's problems. If you drop your phone in a crowded school hallway, you might be surprised that nobody picks it up. Drop it when the hallway isn't crowded, and chances are much better that someone will help. Sometimes we're less likely to help when other people are around; we stand by and assume someone else will swoop in to the rescue. Leaders, however, don't wait.

Inner Workout

- Name three of the most demanding responsibilities you currently have.

- Describe a situation where you decided not to be a bystander and took responsibility for a problem. Now describe a time you didn't.

- When you think about adulthood, what responsibilities are you most excited for? Which scare you? Why?

The same Hillel who said the famous lines at the start of each section of this book also said in Pirkei Avot (Ethics of the Fathers) 2:6, "In a place where there is no person, strive to be a person." We show our humanity when we step up and act. Leaders are the people who volunteer when nobody else does. Leaders give voice to the voiceless, help the helpless, and act proactively. In a crowd of bystanders, leaders are *up*standers. They stand up for what's right, even when they're the only ones who do.

Stella has been invited to a prestigious national conference on social justice that many top college admission delegates attend. To attend, she has to write several essays and commit to attendance at regular webinars. The problem is that she's on responsibility overload. Her single mom works part-time and on weekends, and Stella has to watch her siblings. Her family doesn't have a good support network, and money is very tight. She is already involved in several school clubs, and she is struggling with whether or not she can care for the world while she still has to care for her family.

Challenge: What advice would you give to Stella?

Unlike the age of adulthood in most countries, in Judaism a child becomes bar or bat mitzvah at age twelve or thirteen. At this age, they take on new Jewish responsibilities. In this way, Judaism may help us navigate the transition between being a child and being an adult, incrementally taking on more responsibilities precisely at a time when we think a lot—maybe even *too* much—about ourselves.

Viewed through this lens, the biblical Jonah is portrayed as a person trapped in his own needs, unable to see or take responsibility for the despair of others. God uses nature as a teacher to guide Jonah into thinking about who he wants to be in relation to others, and ultimately stepping up and taking responsibility.

Jewish Bright Spot

The Torah is full of examples of not passively waiting for someone else to take responsibility. For example, Leviticus 19:16 commands us to step up and stand up: "Do not stand idly by when your neighbor's life is at stake."

1. Give an example of a situation when someone's life may literally be at stake. Now give an emotional or spiritual example.

2. Why does the verse stress a "neighbor" instead of, say, a stranger?

3. Describe a time when you probably should have offered help but didn't. How did it make you feel?

34

Prioritizing Leadership

What do you stand for?

Prioritizing means deciding what's most important to us and what we should pay attention to first. The Talmud, for example, sets out clear priorities for giving tzedakah: poor people in your own family come before poor people in your town—who are a higher priority than poor people in another town. Figuring out our priorities is essential because we can't give time and energy to every important cause.

Gabriella, seventeen, is in her final year of high school and takes her leadership responsibilities very seriously. But she's also had to make some important decisions about where to invest her limited time. She felt passionately about several causes: childhood diabetes, climate change, and social justice, to name just a few.

At some point, Gabriella realized that she couldn't be everywhere and fight for everything. She was also a hardworking student, and to balance school work, friends, and her causes, she needed to prioritize her time and do a values check to find an area where she was most interested and could have the most impact.

Ultimately she chose social justice, an area she understood well and felt she could make a meaningful impact by confronting inequality. Energized and impassioned by this decision, Gabriella has been writing op-eds about social justice and attending anti-racist protests, guided by the principle "I understand that I will never understand, but still I stand." She also started a chapter of Girl Up in her school, a movement to advance girls' skills, rights, and opportunities, where she can gather with friends and classmates to confront real-world issues: "As soon as we graduate, we may face real-world violence against women, the kind that people don't really want to talk about."

As Gabriella homed in on where she felt her leadership could really make a difference, she was freed to delve into the work with more enthusiasm rather than feeling torn in several directions: "When I have fifty girls at a meeting and see girls sitting on the floor because we've run out of room, I feel great!" She also enjoys the outreach aspect of social justice, which inspires her to make a better case for what she cares about. "It's a leadership challenge to reach an audience that isn't active in your cause: 'Hey, come join us, come listen, come learn.'" She really loves when girls who formerly didn't care about social justice issues gradually become powerful advocates.

Gabriella hasn't stopped caring about other issues. She has just found what she most loves to work on; achieving positive results has confirmed for her that she made the best choice when it came to prioritizing her time and energy.

Inner Workout

Your class is running a kindness project and your teacher promises to give one hundred dollars to the group that can generate the most positive impact with the money.

Pick one recipient:

- A single mom who can't afford groceries. The money will feed her and her two children for a week.

- A local seniors' facility. It always seems run-down and dreary, and the money will buy art supplies so students can paint and run four weekly craft sessions with residents.

- A Passover food drive. The money could pay for flyers to raise awareness in the community, place collection bins in grocery stores carrying kosher-for-Passover food, and gas money to collect and distribute the food.

- Make-a-Wish. The money will let a local ten-year-old boy with a serious congenital heart condition take a longed-for amusement park trip to enjoy a normal day of fun with his family.

One thing that helped Gabriella prioritize her social justice work was taking an honest look at her values, supported by Jewish teachings, such as texts that mention the plight of the vulnerable, like helping out the widow, the orphan, and the stranger. "I love learning *Tanach* [Bible] in school, and when I find something that inspires me—when I see lines that already exist that prove our obligation—then it helps." Ancient words and wisdom stir her commitment to tikun olam and inspire her to think about working on behalf of vulnerable groups.

Gabriella spent time thinking through her choices when it came to prioritizing her leadership. What about you? How can the vision and mission statements we created in part I of this book help you prioritize your leadership activities? What Jewish teachings are going to guide you?

Use the following blank lines (or as many as you need) to write down every club, cause, and organization you're involved with—no matter how much or how little time you give each one.

Now that you've written down all your activities, you can prioritize them. Put the number "1" next to the activity that you are most enthusiastic about and most want to be involved with. Continue numbering the activities until you get to "10," the activity that means the least to you.

Now review your list and ask yourself these two questions:

- What should I be doing more of?

- What should I be doing less of?

Jewish Bright Spot

The prophet Isaiah says, "Learn to do good: seek justice, relieve the oppressed, judge the fatherless, plead for the widow." (Isaiah 1:17) The word *learn* suggests that goodness is not always obvious, nor can we assume that people will gravitate toward goodness. Sometimes it needs to be taught.

1. What good do we have to learn to do? Doesn't it come naturally?

2. Why do you think this verse presents a few ways to do good?

3. As you prioritize your goals in leadership, what would you add to Isaiah's list?

35

Turning Problems into Possibilities

Ben had taken on other leadership roles before he started his own basketball camp when he was fifteen. That's what taught him the most about leadership, he says, largely through problem-solving: "The basketball camp was challenging for me at the start. It was hard to get kids and then make sure they were having a good time."

Ben was engaged in the leadership components of creating any good cohort program: doing recruitment, helping kids treat each other respectfully, and encouraging his team not to give up even when they were losing. He loved bringing out the best in an "underdog" player or celebrating an unexpected win. But it wasn't all wins, and sometimes Ben had to learn how to transform a mistake into a learning moment.

One day, for example, Ben simply could not get through to a particular camper. "This kid gets in trouble a lot because he doesn't like to play by rules," Ben explains. "He's on his phone. He doesn't do his drills." Ben had spoken to the boy before and tried to help him become a better, more engaged team player. One day, Ben saw that one of the other players was really upset. Someone had made fun of him; Ben immediately concluded that it had been the "troublemaker." He lost it.

"I yelled very harshly at the kid who was making trouble," Ben admits. "But it turned out to be the wrong kid. I felt terrible. It was really bad." Ben had to work his way out of a poor judgment call, and there was no referee to answer to except his own conscience. "I judged it way too fast," he says.

Regret wasn't enough. Ben still had to deal with the boy's bruised feelings No one likes to be unfairly accused, especially in front of friends. He needed a solution—fast.

- Describe a problem that happened while you were leading that you still think about.

- Describe your feelings about it at the time.

- How did you handle it?

- How do you feel and think about that problem now?

As soon as Ben realized he'd accused the wrong boy, he talked to him in private: "I sat him down and said, 'I'm sorry. I shouldn't have treated you that way. I have no business yelling at you. Or anybody, for that matter.'"

Ben had been so overconfident that he let his leadership guard down and rushed to judgment. In his anger, he ended up making a person he was trying to grow feel really small. He says this also showed another problem as well: a lack of compassion. "When you're leading, you need to be emotionally connected to the kids. In the moment, I messed up because I yelled at a kid and didn't think twice about it. I wasn't compassionate. I needed to believe in the kids I was leading."

But Ben's actions had further repercussions. All the other players were aware of his mistake and were watching him to see how he'd handle the situation. *Ouch.* "Being a leader isn't like turning a switch," he says. "You can be cursing, hanging out, being negligent, not aware that you're being watched. You can't turn on and turn off a 'leadership switch.' You need to be on all the time."

Ben knew he'd have to work to fix his mistake: rebuilding trust with the entire team, particularly the boy he'd accused. He worked extra hard to win back the boy's trust. "I had to convince him that I wasn't that bad of a guy," Ben says. "When you're in power, you can assert your authority to make sure others behave. In that moment, I could have used my power a lot better, and I was not the most responsible I've ever been."

Just as Ben managed to transform a mishandled situation into an opportunity for growth, there are many ways leaders can reframe problems through honesty, self-reflection, and change. In the next chapter, we'll explore some practical ways to accomplish this, overcoming mistakes and learning from them to become better leaders.

Jewish Bright Spot

The Talmudic sage Rabbi Yohanan taught his students that a community should appoint a leader "only if he has a box full of creeping animals hanging behind him." By this he meant something unsavory or unpleasant in the leader's past—metaphorical demons; unresolved issues hanging around that aren't pretty. That way, if a leader ever starts boasting or abusing their power, others can point to their past to keep them humble.

1. Rabbi Yohanan was an important leader in his time. Do you think that being a rabbi community leader makes it easier or harder to admit your own mistakes?

2. When is it safe to keep that "box full of creeping animals" open and when is it best to keep it shut?

EMBRACE YOUR MISTAKES

Every leader is bound to make mistakes. Yet mistakes can be our greatest teachers, as Ben learned in the previous chapter. This explains why the Torah, far from hiding the mistakes of Jewish heroes and role models, is full of stories of moral weakness, because no matter how good or righteous someone is, they will never be perfect. The struggle to repair mistakes is the story of all great leaders. We are all human and flawed, as Jewish wisdom reminds us: "Indeed, there is no one on earth who is righteous, who does what is right and never sins." (Ecclesiastes 7:20)

In the previous chapter we talked about transforming problems into opportunities. In this chapter we'll explore ways to create a leadership culture that embraces mistakes for the sake of growth. "Making mistakes is a good way of learning, and good leaders talk about mistakes they've made," says Matt Grossman, who began as a teen leader with NFTY and is now the CEO of BBYO. Participating in a youth group took him to places outside his small town in Connecticut and provided social opportunities. By the time he was on the regional board, he'd become convinced of the importance of activism and social justice. Grossman compared his mistakes and how he handled them to the way athletes improve over time. "You can have talent, but then there's training," he says. We might handle the mistakes of leadership easier if we labeled them as training.

In his book *Gateway to Self-Knowledge*, Rabbi Zelig Pliskin presents dozens of questions to help you think through an approach to mistake-making. Here are a few:

- What is your usual reaction when you make a mistake?

- Do you spend a large amount of time berating yourself for your mistakes? If so, what do you lose by doing so?

- When other people point out your mistakes to you, are you usually: (a) grateful, (b) angry at them, or (c) embarrassed?

- In what ways do you view mistakes as learning experiences to help you grow?

- When you make mistakes, do you carefully analyze the reasons for your mistakes?

- Can you think of a mistake you made that led to a very positive outcome?

Once, when chatting with a group of youth leaders, Grossman asked what they liked about the program. One said that in every other part of his life, adults tell him what to do. Within his youth movement, on the other hand, he felt more empowered: "Every adult tells me to listen to my own voice: 'How are you going to solve this? What do you think?'"

For Grossman, one of the great joys of his role is watching young leaders overcome their mistakes. The organization helps by creating safe spaces where they can name and reflect on their mistakes together: evaluating where teamwork has broken down; assessing a program that didn't achieve its objectives or fixing technical problems with logistics so things will run better next time.

Practice Makes Perfect

Here are six steps that can help you process a leadership mistake and transform it into a learning experience:

1. Name your mistake before someone else does.

2. Own it.

3. Acknowledge who has been affected by your mistake and apologize.

4. Talk about the steps you're taking to fix the mistake you made.

5. Seek input from others.

6. Show others how you've learned from your mistake.

The legendary basketball coach Dean Smith used to give his players four simple steps if they made a mistake: "Recognize it, admit it, learn from it, forget it." He didn't say it was easy to forget your mistakes. But he knew that if you don't let them go, they can cripple you. In life, as in basketball, you are not your worst mistake. Your successes define you more than your failures.

Taking the time to process and analyze mistakes as a group makes it easier for everyone to take responsibility. Talking about mistakes becomes more comfortable and natural. Evaluating an event or program also allows everyone to celebrate successes together and name and assess what's working well. We don't spend enough time catching people being good and doing good. When we work really hard, we need to pause and high-five each other.

Jewish Bright Spot

Rabbi Samson Raphael Hirsch (1808–1888), an intellectual who worked to reconcile traditional Jewish practice with modern Enlightenment ideas, pointed out in his commentary on Genesis that "[t]he Torah never hides from us the faults, errors, and weaknesses of our great people." He believed this made its message more authentic and resonant for us than if it attempted to sugarcoat the truth. "If they stood before us as the purest models of perfection we should attribute them as having a different nature, which has been denied to us. Were they without passion, without internal struggle, their virtues would seem to us the outcome of some higher nature, hardly a merit and certainly no model that we could hope to emulate."

1. What do you think Rabbi Hirsch means by this? Why does the Torah deliberately show leaders' flaws?

2. When has a leader let you down in some way—yet you still think of them as a role model?

3. Describe a time when you let someone down as a leader.

37

Innovation Nation

Innovation is usually the result of trial and error, hard work, mistakes, and experimentation. Gertrude Elion, who won the Nobel Prize in 1988 for her discovery of a range of drugs to fight cancer, AIDS, and other viruses, once said, "Don't let others discourage you, or tell you that you can't do it. In my day I was told women didn't go into chemistry. I saw no reason why we couldn't." Just as Elion dared to challenge attitudes about women in science that weren't working, she used experimentation in her research to challenge ideas that didn't work. For instance, many scientists doubted drugs would ever be able to fight viruses; Elion and others proved them wrong.

Innovators work through conversation, collaboration, or reexamination of old ideas in new ways, sometimes filling a void we never knew we had. Back in the 1970s, Steve Jobs, the cofounder of Apple, began asking how he could make computers accessible to people at home. Before that, most people didn't even think they needed a computer at home. Good ideas need constant reworking. Good leadership works the same way.

As the editor of his high school's yearbook and weekly newsletter, Ariel had mastered the basic technical skills he needed to do the job. "The newsletter was totally student-run, with some faculty help, and it went out to the entire school community." But with the same newsletter format coming out week after week, things had gotten stale, to the point where nobody read the newsletter. On a quest to improve and innovate, Ariel led his team in a new creative initiative. He picked up some new skills and reinvented the newsletter in an exciting video format that got everyone's attention. "We didn't want things to stay the same because we have to keep people interested. That boosted our creativity. We made something static into something interactive." The result was a huge hit: five years later, many of the techniques Ariel's team innovated are still in use.

Once Ariel got to university, this experience innovating gave him the courage to take more risks with Israel events on campus. Pro-Israel programming had become predictable and dull, but Ariel already knew that livening it up with new ideas would attract new audiences and set a higher standard—making the events more fun and meaningful for everybody involved, reflecting the group's enthusiasm for Israel advocacy.

In college, Ariel was excited to have more autonomy and authority to develop creative, exciting events. He also realized it was essential to innovate because he was competing for students' interest with so many other campus groups. "I always asked myself, 'How do I apply what they're doing to what we're doing and grow from that?'"

Inner Workout

- Name one invention that has changed your life for the better.

- Describe a change that you helped bring about that's made someone's life better.

- What's an innovation you'd like to bring about in your leadership? Don't hold back. Dream. Now dream bigger!

Not everything you do has to be different or original. As a religion that is thousands of years old, Judaism has had to continuously blend innovation and tradition, asking questions about how ancient practices and beliefs can guide us in handling modern scientific, cultural, and social developments. Is artificially cultured meat kosher? Are the latest medical advances compatible with Jewish ethical principles? What guidance can Jewish wisdom offer to Israel's modern court system? Questions like these stimulate new and original answers while honoring the beauty of tradition.

And of course, no matter what you do, *you* are original. There is no one else like you. That itself is an innovation. So think about how you express your originality in the world and what you want to contribute that is unique and rewarding.

The Talmud states that every person should be aware that "the world was created for me." Taking this idea even further, a statement attributed to Rabbi Nachman of Breslov (1772–1810) says, "The day you were born is the day God decided the world could not exist without you." The world needs you.

Jewish Bright Spot

The Lubavitcher Rebbe, Rabbi Menachem Mendel Schneerson (1902–1994), once said, "If you see what needs to be repaired and you know how to repair it, then you have found a piece of the world that God has left for you to perfect. But if you only see what is wrong and what is ugly, then it is you yourself that needs repair."

1. What do you think Rabbi Schneerson means that God has left something for you to perfect?

2. In what way do you see yourself partnering with God in changing the world?

3. If you find yourself seeing lots of ugliness in the world, how would you go about changing yourself?

38

THE TECH TRAP

Social media interactions can feel like a page out of *Lord of the Flies*. In this novel, a group of English boys are stranded on an island without any adults, and the consequences are disastrous. The boys fight over power and use violence to get their way. Today, technology has created exactly this scenario for many teens: a virtual island with little adult supervision. Technology offers so many advantages—including new and exciting ways to communicate, network, and reach larger audiences than ever before—but at the same time, its potential to create harm can be terrifying. Teens suffer belittling and bullying. Their secrets are exposed. Their privacy is breached. And sometimes things get so bad that, just like in *Lord of the Flies*, precious lives are lost.

Polls show that most teens have positive feelings about the effect of social media. Jessa, from Johannesburg, South Africa, says technology helps her stay connected to people she cares about and offers "a release from everyday life and reality." On the other hand, Jessa is concerned that "everything that is posted is out there for the world to see." She also worries that social media in particular can trap us in a never-ending loop of insecurity:

> People spend hours looking at pictures of the lives of others—wishing they could be more like them. . . . It can often waste hours of one's time, draining one's energy and not refilling oneself with anything of value.

For Jessa, using technology responsibly means "shedding light on topics that the world needs to see and spreading awareness of ideas or promoting learning." That's the way to harness technology for leadership: letting others know about events, causes, and issues.

Alex, from Auckland, New Zealand, says that technology helped her find a safe space while she was figuring out who she was and what she cared about. She was able to find online support groups and ask questions anonymously on issues she was exploring. "In terms of identity and sexuality, and from the perspective of someone who is part of the LGBTQ+ community, I believe social media has played a really big part in encouraging parts of people that could otherwise have gone suppressed for the rest of their lives."

Like Jessa, Alex uses technology to keep up on current events and express her activism on behalf of causes she supports. However, living in Auckland, where many of her friends and media followers are not Jewish, Alex believes that Jewish activism is particularly important. Alex volunteers for a support line that is purely text-based because, as she explained to us, it's a more natural medium for teens to share their experiences than over the phone or in person. This is a great example of how technology has created a platform for networking and constructing communities of understanding and compassion.

Inner Workout

- How has technology helped *your* leadership?

- When has something you've texted or posted had a visible, positive impact on others?

- Describe a time you felt your own values were compromised because of a text or post.

Alex says she's also deeply concerned about the flood of false information available online, especially when it comes to hate speech. It's not only about how fast lies and fake news travel but also the way it influences how she sees herself. Like Jessa, Alex admits to a deep concern with how others perceive her via social media:

There's an underlying pressure to create a picture-perfect-looking life. . . . I try not to let it consume me but that is a downfall, and sometimes it's hard to not compare yourself to others, when in reality life isn't nearly that perfect.

Alex believes social media encourages people to share intimate details that might be healthier not to share. As an anonymous teen we spoke with said,

I believe there is a correlation with the spread of social media and the rise in sexual experimentation. Social media and what teens are exposed to these days often sends off the message of "anything goes." There is no limit or restriction to "being yourself."

This may be even more true because, just like in *Lord of the Flies*, adults have virtually no presence in most teens' online lives. Parents and teachers can rarely intervene to stop bullying or check if a post is appropriate. In some ways, this distance is healthy: teens need privacy. It's impossible to discover who you really are if all your decisions and relationships are controlled by adults.

How can you, as a teen leader, model constructive, responsible technology use? Here are a few ideas and suggestions that might help:

- It's great to relax with social media, but set time limits and stick to them.

- Use social media to drive support for issues and acts of kindness.

- Call out harsh, unfiltered language when you see it, especially if it's bullying.

- Use social media to create positive communities that build genuine self-esteem by praising and complimenting.

- Thank someone who makes positive, constructive use of social media to help others.

There is a midrash (a rabbinic storytelling tradition that explains or interprets biblical events) about a conversation between God and Adam after the world was created. God showed Adam all the fruit trees, animals, and other beautiful aspects of this new world: "Look at My creations, how beautiful and praiseworthy they are. And I have created all of it for your sake. Contemplate this and be watchful that you do not damage or destroy My world. For if you damage it, there will be no one else to repair it after you." (*Kohelet Rabbah* 7:28)

1. What kind of damage could humans do to the world that could not be repaired?

2. How would you apply this message to technology today?

3. What are ways you can repair some of the dangers of technology in your own life?

39

END BULLYING

Whether it takes place online or offline, bullying hurts. It also undermines the good work you're doing as a leader by fostering environments where people feel unhappy or unprotected. The website Stopbullying.gov defines bullying by its three core elements:

- Unwanted aggressive behavior

- Observed or perceived power imbalance

- Repetition or high likelihood of repetition of bullying behaviors

Victims of bullying feel sad, alone, isolated, unworthy, and distressed. They can experience paralyzing low self-esteem. When left unchecked, bullying can even kill, as we've seen from high-profile headlines where teens are driven to suicide by online rumors, inappropriate photos, or cruel comments. Perhaps this is what the Bible means when it says, "Death and life are in the power of the tongue." (Proverbs 18:21)

Do you have the courage to stand up for someone who is being bullied? Many teens today are involved with large social justice causes but still don't intervene when someone they know is being picked on. Pirkei Avot (Ethics of the Fathers) 4:12 states that "your friend's dignity should be as precious to you as your own." How do you react when someone is being bullied, especially in the presence of others?

- Describe a time when you were bullied or witnessed someone else being bullied. Dig deep. Describe the incident in detail, from where it took place to what you were wearing, the time of day, words exchanged, and how you felt at the time.

- Think of an incident when someone you know was bullied. Describe it.

- Now alter the scenario and explain what you *could have* done or said differently in that moment.

About 20 percent of students experience some form of bullying, often at school but also online, in social settings, and at work. It can be verbal, physical, or sexual.

Bullies treat people as objects to be teased, kicked, and pushed around. It's easy to mistake bullying for leadership because bullies can be loud, manipulative, hold power, and attract followers. But make no mistake: bullying is the opposite of true leadership. It shows profound disrespect and irresponsibility. And bullies aren't the only ones responsible. People who support them or fail to confront them are also partly to blame.

Many people assume that bullying is a natural part of childhood, but it doesn't have to be. Everyone is entitled to a happy, bully-free childhood. Be warned: Bullies often grow up to continue bullying. It's a behavior some adults never outgrow. Here's where you come in.

Jewish Bright Spot

According to the Talmud, we're all responsible for stopping anyone within our circles of influence from doing harm: "Whoever can prevent members of his household from committing a wrongdoing, but does not, is punished for the wrongdoings of his household; whoever can prevent fellow citizens from committing a wrongdoing but does not, is punished for the wrongdoings of his fellow citizens; whoever can prevent the whole world from committing a wrongdoing, but does not, is punished for the wrongdoings of the whole world."

1. Why do you think this text puts so much of the burden for wrongdoings of others on a single individual?

2. Can you think of a wrongdoing in your family, community, and world that you can prevent, even in a small way?

3. How would you relate this text to the problem of bullying?

40

Taking the Lead Against Antisemitism

Throughout history, different people have been targets of hate based on their skin color, religion, or nationality. Even as we fight alongside those who are marginalized and persecuted from all backgrounds, we also recognize that as Jews, we too have been subjected to hate for millennia. At its worst, this hate took the form of the Holocaust, but Jews also suffered through the Crusades, the Inquisition, enslavement, and pogroms.

Though every group has its own story, it is important that we know our own and can sound the alarm when antisemitism rears its ugly face, as it did on October 27, 2018, when an intruder entered the Tree of Life Synagogue in Pittsburgh, Pennsylvania, and murdered eleven people, including six Holocaust survivors. It was the deadliest attack on the Jewish community that has ever taken place in the United States.

"Before the Tree of Life murders," says Jack, a fifteen-year-old from Morristown, New Jersey, "I didn't really think that antisemitism still existed. After the shooting, I realized that it still does." But Jack later admitted that years before the massacre, vandals had scrawled swastikas on his middle school's walls. Perhaps, like many of us, he hadn't wanted to see this "minor" antisemitic act as part of a more serious and widespread problem.

No one wants to believe that hate has as much power as it does. So we "forget" an antisemitic comment or joke, ignore the hurt of an ignorant statement, or flip past bad news in the newspaper to the sports section. We might do the same for a racist or misogynist comment.

Even if you've never personally experienced antisemitism, you can't deny the facts, the data, or the urgency of fighting antisemitism.

Antisemitism has been called the oldest form of hatred. In the story of Purim, which took place around the fifth century BCE, Queen Esther's uncle Mordechai refused to bow down to Haman, one of the king's chief ministers. In revenge, Haman justified the killing of Mordechai and all his people—the Jews—by telling King Ahasuerus that the Jews were *different*: "There is a certain people, scattered and dispersed among the other peoples in all the provinces of your realm, whose laws are different from those of any other people." (Esther 3:8) This story of persecution has repeated itself throughout Jewish history. Despite scientific and social progress, the virus of antisemitism persists and continues to mutate.

Inner Workout

- Have you ever personally experienced antisemitism? If so, describe it.

- What may be uncomfortable about combating antisemitism?

- Name some concrete steps you can take to combat antisemitism today.

So what should we do about this virus of irrational hate? The journalist Bari Weiss offers several suggestions in her book *How to Fight Anti-Semitism*:

- **Tell the truth.** Many people—including many Jews—want to deny the extent of antisemitism. We can't, and we shouldn't.

- **Trust your discomfort.** If you find yourself feeling uncomfortable in a setting simply because you are Jewish, trust your instincts. "Since when is being a fun guest at a dinner party more important than standing up for what matters?" Weiss asks. And when you speak up, she says, be sure to criticize *ideas*, not identities.

- **Apply the *kippah* (or Magen David) test.** Weiss had her bat mitzvah at the Tree of Life Synagogue in Pittsburgh. After the massacre there in 2018, she began openly wearing a Magen David necklace. "This show of pride has become important to me. I want people to know that I am unafraid," she explains. One of the best ways to confront hate is to own your identity.

Case Study

On his way to Hebrew school, Emanuel, thirteen, is passing through his synagogue's parking lot when a group of boys walking past start throwing pennies at him and calling him a cheap Jew. Shaken, Emanuel reports what had happened to the rabbi as well as to his Hebrew school teacher, who suggests that he use the experience to create a program for the class.

Challenge: What advice would you give to Emanuel?

Even if you've never been a victim of antisemitism directly, as a Jewish leader, you're in a unique position to take meaningful action, calling out this form of hatred in small and large ways. So what can *you* do right now?

- Start a social media campaign to promote Jewish organizations you care about and positive Jewish values.

- Take meaningful sayings from prominent Jews and Jewish sources and publicize them in visible places.

- If an antisemitic incident occurs in your community, write to the relevant public figures to show concern and raise awareness.

- Contribute time and money to nonprofit organizations that protect and defend Jews everywhere.

Fighting antisemitism isn't just about defending Jews; it's about preserving freedom for all types of people. According to the Holocaust historian Dr. Deborah Lipstadt, antisemitism is a wake-up call to all of us. "Antisemitism flourishes in a society that is intolerant of others, be they immigrants or racial and religious minorities," she writes. "When expressions of contempt for one group become normative, it is virtually inevitable that similar hatred will be directed at other groups." Hatred in society may begin with antisemitism, but it never ends there.

While Jewish history is filled with stories of persecution, it also offers so many stories of triumph and meaning. There is plenty of cause for hope: we're still here. In Daniella Levy's historical novel *By Light of Hidden Candles*, set during the Spanish Inquisition, she writes that Jews throughout history have stubbornly clung to life and joy "even in the face of horror and death":

> Our story is not only about exile and oppression and suffering. It is the story of thriving, of triumph, and of great faith. . . . We take our pain and turn it into poetry. We take our misfortune and transform it into opportunity.

It's not always easy to transform misfortune into opportunity. But fighting hate in the form of antisemitism will help us empathize with others confronting irrational hate, racism, or discrimination. When we stand up and talk back, we find the inner strength and the voice to build a more just society—not just for Jews but for everyone, everywhere.

Remember: the best way to combat hatred of Jews is by living proudly as a Jew.

Jewish Bright Spot

On the festival of Shavuot, we read the book of Ruth, about a Moabite princess who leaves her comfortable home for a difficult life as a Jew in Bethlehem. To support herself and her mother-in-law, Ruth gathers scraps from the harvest of a wealthy man. She finds it difficult to accept his kindnesses, bowing down and asking him, "Why are you so kind as to single me out, when I am a foreigner?" (Ruth 2:10)

1. Why do you think Ruth feels so isolated?

2. Just as Ruth was surprised by the kindness of a stranger, many Jews have internalized antisemitism. How does this impact how we think of ourselves?

3. We discussed bullying in the previous chapter. What are some ways bullying and antisemitism are similar—or different?

41

YOUR I.Q. (ISRAEL QUOTIENT)

Israel has served as the spiritual center for Jews for thousands of years. It is where the two Temples once stood and where prophets walked. Traditionally, Jews have prayed for Israel, directed their prayers toward Jerusalem, fasted over tragedies, yearned for religious freedom, and rejoiced at the opportunity to have their own state and government. After two thousand years, Jews finally have a place to call home and have built the only democracy in the Middle East.

Of course, Israel is far from perfect. There is a long journey to regional stability ahead. Israel has become a highly politicized topic, and some see supporting Israel and Zionism as controversial. Many of us struggle to understand our own relationship with Israel or feel shame over Israeli government policies. You may have experienced criticism from friends or classmates or heard about anti-Israel sentiment on a local college campus or a rally against Israel in your community. It's hard to make sense of the competing claims and complex ethical issues at play.

All of this may leave you unsure of your feelings. David Ben Gurion, Israel's first prime minister, understood that Israel's existence would forever change the way we and others see being Jewish: "Israel has created a new image of the Jew in the world—the image of a working and an intellectual people, of a people that can fight with heroism."

One of the challenges is that we often don't know enough about the challenges Israel faces to answer our own questions and those of others. We dream of Israel as a homeland we can be proud of but also acknowledge that, just like all countries, Israel often struggles to live up to this dream. Nevertheless, we can still love a place despite certain disappointments, and we can channel that feeling constructively to advocate for change.

● If you've been to Israel, describe a memory. If you haven't visited Israel, where would you most like to visit, and why?

● What historic event involving Israel is most meaningful to you?

The modern State of Israel has provided refuge after millennia of exile for Jews from all over the world—including more than half of the survivors of the devastation of the Holocaust and the vast majority of Jews living under persecution in surrounding Arab countries. Today, Jews continue to arrive from places where they face violence and intolerance, such as the former Soviet Union, India, and Ethiopia. To quote the historian Paul Johnson, "In the past half-century, more than one hundred new independent states have come into existence. Israel is the only one whose creation can fairly be called a miracle."

And who made so much of this happen? Teen leaders.

Many of the pioneers who built and protected the state began as idealistic members of youth movements long before statehood was officially declared in 1948. They influenced communal organizations, education, and political awareness. They orchestrated Jewish resistance in ghettoes and concentration camps. They turned dreams and ideas into actions. They built the kibbutz movement and educational centers from the ground up. They fought in wars, drained swamps, invested in infrastructure, and learned to build a country.

How much do you know about Israel? What's your I.Q. (Israel quotient)? Take our I.Q. test and discuss what you know about the following:

Name a few major events in Israeli history:

Name as many political parties in Israel as you can:

Name a few Israeli songs and bands:

Name a few Israeli novels or novelists:

Name as many Israeli cities as you can:

Give yourself one point for every answer you were able to give in every category. How did you do?

When Avi, fifteen, was a sophomore in high school in South Florida, he got involved with the American Israel Public Affairs Committee (AIPAC) through his synagogue. Avi started informing himself about Israeli life and politics and learned how to advocate for Israel by writing to members of local government and Congress. Avi says, "Even though I couldn't vote, I could still have some say in writing letters. I was making phone calls and sending emails."

Avi understands that you can love a place and still not love every aspect of that place. For example, you don't have to agree with everything the Israeli prime minister says or does. As Avi sees it, local politicians and leaders aren't always right either: "You don't have to agree with the government to support the country."

For many Jews all over the world—from Spain, France, Ethiopia, Syria, Australia, the United States, and every other country from where Jews have made *aliyah*—Israel is like a big, noisy table full of family members: couples, siblings, and distant cousins. We don't all agree (nor should we); we don't even always get along, but we still feel connected to each other and at times—especially at difficult times—show up for each other.

Jewish teen leaders have to be prepared to discuss some of the tense political issues that surround Israel in an informed, respectful, and nonjudgmental way. Constructive criticism is fundamental and necessary for any healthy democracy. But if our entire relationship is only built on criticism, then it's not really a relationship. We can also acknowledge and celebrate Israeli accomplishments in science, medicine, technology, music, art, food, and in so many other areas.

Legend has it that someone once asked Chaim Weizmann, Israel's first president, why the Jews insisted on having their state in the biblical land of Israel instead of an undeveloped country somewhere else. Weizmann responded, "That is like my asking you why you

drove twenty miles to visit your mother last Sunday when there are so many old ladies living on your street." People are people, but family is different. Land is land, but not every place feels like a homeland.

Knowing more about Israel will help you be more informed about issues and help you develop your own relationship with Israel.

Jewish Bright Spot

Golda Meir (1898–1978) was Israel's fourth prime minister, but her leadership career began in the fourth grade. When poor children in her neighborhood of Milwaukee, Wisconsin, couldn't afford new textbooks, Meir and her friends stepped up to form the American Young Sisters Society, raising money to help buy textbooks. As a teen, Meir was influenced by debates between her older sister and her sister's husband about Zionism, literature, and trade unionism. In her autobiography, she later wrote, "To the extent that my own future convictions were shaped and given form . . . those talk-filled nights in Denver played a considerable role."

1. What part of your leadership involvement now might one day appear in your autobiography?

2. Are there any conversations you've overheard that inspired you to get involved?

3. How does Israel shape your Jewish consciousness?

42

JUDAISM AND RACIAL JUSTICE

Here's one of the most hurtful things you can say to someone who shows up at your synagogue or youth group: "Funny, you don't look Jewish." Really? Is there only *one* way to look Jewish? If the modern State of Israel has taught us anything it's that Jews come in all colors, sizes, and ethnic backgrounds. Because of this, we have a special obligation to create an even playing field for people of all races, as the Torah mandates by emphasizing the infinite worth of every human being. We all share in that job—protecting and honoring one another—but leaders have an additional role to play in advocating, amplifying, and creating a vision of justice for others to follow.

This was something that Rabbi Abraham Joshua Heschel (1907–1972) understood implicitly. On June 16, 1963, Rabbi Heschel, who would later march arm in arm with the Reverend Martin Luther King Jr., sent a telegram urging President John F. Kennedy to support the fight for civil rights and to declare a state of "moral emergency." Racial injustice, he wrote, was like the weather: "Everybody talks about it but nobody does anything about it. Please demand of religious leaders personal involvement, not just solemn declaration. . . . The hour calls for moral grandeur and spiritual audacity."

As part of the American Jewish Committee Leaders for Tomorrow training program (AJCLFT) as well as her student council, Eyden, sixteen, wants to do something about it. Eyden doesn't always tell people she's biracial, but she doesn't hide it either. For the most part, she says, "It hasn't been difficult to be in a Jewish day school as a biracial student." But sometimes her intersectional identity means she notices incidents and comments that others might not. For example, during a class about the Jim Crow laws and racial protests in the southern US, a classmate made a disparaging comment about Black people.  The teacher immediately stepped in, but Eyden felt hurt and targeted, especially because no other students noticed or pointed out the problem. Eyden says:

Am I a Jew of color? Yes and no. Yeah, I'm just like everybody else, but when somebody says something like a racial joke or a comment, then I feel it. I feel like they're not thinking about what they're saying.

Eyden hopes to expand her Jewish leadership to bring together her identities and her interests. She'd love to create a coalition among organizations working with both Jewish and Black populations to fix some of the problems she sees in the ways these groups interact and in the ways Jews of color experience the world.

Jews of color should not have to fight this battle alone. The educational psychologist and antiracist activist Dr. Deitra Reiser says, "I want more people to be invested in the antiracist community. If there is one thing we have learned over the last few years it is that not being racist is not good enough. We must work—do the hard work—of being antiracist."

Creating a big tent means we all need to stand up to bigotry. Yet sometimes our efforts to promote diversity and inclusion can open a Pandora's box of emotions. Race conversations can quickly become filled with anger, righteous indignation, and misunderstanding caused by understandably strong feelings. Be careful when raising issues about race; check in with those who might feel victimized to see and hear what their needs are.

Inner Workout

- What does your youth movement, synagogue, or organization do to welcome and create belonging for Jews of color?

- What are you doing personally to create greater racial justice?

Becoming part of the solution, according to Dr. Reiser, means becoming proactive and being willing to change ourselves. "Start now and start with I," she says. Here are some suggestions from Dr. Reiser and others to help leaders build racial equality:

1. Be aware of your own biases. "We all have them," says Dr. Reiser. Identify your own biased thoughts and actions and root them out.

2. Speak up when someone makes a racist comment or joke. Speak out when there are racist incidents in your school, neighborhood, or community, and reach out to any individuals or communities near you who might have been affected. They need to hear that you noticed and care.

3. Collaborate with other organizations and communities actively working to defeat racism. As Dr. Reiser says, "Individuals change organizations and institutions, which, in turn, change society."

4. Lean into the discomfort, writes Jordan Daniels, a Jew of color who used to avoid difficult talks around race. "Now I've deliberately decided to lean into these uncomfortable situations instead of avoiding them, and . . . I've discovered that these situations are opportunities to teach and learn."

Rabbi Angela Warnick Buchdahl, the senior rabbi of New York's Central Synagogue, felt alone growing up in the Jewish community. "My sister and I were . . . the only ones with Asian faces, the only ones whose family trees didn't have roots in Eastern Europe, the only ones with kimchee on the seder plate," she explains. Tired of feeling like she constantly had to prove herself, she decided to give up being Jewish, but ultimately she realized that "I could no sooner stop being a Jew than I could stop being Korean, or female, or me." Leaning into her identity, she began studying Judaism and now draws strength from the diversity of the Jewish community: "Walking through the streets of modern-day Israel, one sees the multicolored faces of Ethiopian, Russian, Yemenite, Iraqi, Moroccan, Polish, and countless other races of Jews." Just as Rabbi Buchdahl learned to honor and develop fully all parts of her identity, the communities where we lead must do the same.

Jewish Bright Spot

Jewish tradition teaches us that we must reach beyond our community, loving and caring for people who are not like us specifically *because* they are not like us:

- "The stranger who resides with you shall be to you as one of your citizens; you shall love them as yourself, for you were strangers in the land of Egypt." (Leviticus 19:34)

- "You shall not wrong a stranger or oppress them, for you were strangers in the land of Egypt." (Exodus 22:20)

- "You shall have one standard for stranger and citizen alike: for I Adonai am your God." (Leviticus 24:22)

- "You shall not subvert the rights of the stranger or the fatherless; you shall not take a widow's garment in pawn." (Deuteronomy 24:17)

1. What do all these verses have in common?

2. What differences do you notice among these verses?

3. Describe a personal experience you've had that has helped you be more empathetic or understanding toward "strangers" (of any kind; anyone who is "not like you" in some way).

43

INCLUSION AND DIVERSITY

In the previous chapter, we talked about how you can help ensure racial justice within your leadership role. But inclusion doesn't stop with race; it also means ensuring your group is open and accessible to a broad range of people, regardless of disability, gender, sexual orientation, and social or cultural background.

The Torah lays the groundwork for inclusion in Leviticus 19:14, where we are told not to put a stumbling block before the blind. We can understand this metaphorically: we are not supposed to take advantage of people or intentionally put barriers before them. But we can also read this biblical command quite literally. In what ways do we not accommodate people with disabilities by not making spaces and events accessible? We came away inspired after speaking with Batya, a high-schooler who's blind. She prays from a Braille siddur (prayer book), studies using a Braille Bible, and participates in Jewish life because thoughtful people understood that Batya deserves the same access to Jewish life as her friends.

Creating equal opportunities for people with disabilities is our job. When it comes to disabilities, inclusion means making sure that physical spaces are accessible and that all events and programs we organize as leaders accommodate people with a range of physical, emotional, and intellectual needs.

In her memoir *Being Heumann: An Unrepentant Memoir of a Disability Rights Activist*, Judy Heumann, who had polio as a child and uses a wheelchair, writes that she was often given the implicit message that her needs were too burdensome for others. Her local school principal refused to let her register for kindergarten, for example, claiming she was a "fire hazard." She says people with disabilities are often made to feel "that asking for an equal opportunity is asking for too much."

Heumann's experiences have inspired her to create disability awareness and change laws to even the playing field. In recognition of her accomplishments, President Barack Obama appointed her special advisor for international disability rights in 2010.

Inner Workout

- Think about a time when you felt excluded and describe the scene in as much physical and emotional detail as you can.

- Pick one physical disability and write a paragraph imagining what everyday activities are like through the lens of what you cannot do rather than what you can.

- What have you done as a leader to make an experience more accessible and inclusive?

Beyond disability, inclusion also means working to ensure that our schools, businesses, places of government, and organizations are truly welcoming to people from a range of social and ethnic backgrounds, genders, sexual orientations, disabilities, and other groups. Within the Jewish community, we can strive for inclusion by honoring the story and presence of all Jews and acknowledging the many Jewish portals to participation without judging them. People find Jewish meaning in observing laws and traditions, philanthropy, Israel, equality, sustainability, and economic and racial justice. From a Jewish leadership perspective, inclusion also means making sure committees and boards within our organizations have fair and equal representation.

Case Study

Kayla and her three best friends all live a few blocks apart in Manchester, England. One day, a new girl named Meriam joins their class. Meriam has autism. She seems comfortable with the academic work and tests, but her comments in class sometimes sound strange and off-putting. Sometimes she leaves class for enrichment programs. Kayla's best friends, like everyone else in class, have a silent agreement to stay away from the new girl. Despite her friends' behavior, Kayla recognizes how alienating Meriam's experience of school must be; she just doesn't know how to make the situation better.

Challenge: What advice would you give to Kayla?

Jordyn, who was the victim of character attacks that made her feel marginalized, found her voice in high school as a leader in her local youth movement. A naturally shy person, she used that leadership role to bring in anyone on the margins or who looked uncomfortable or out of place:

> A Jewish value that has always influenced my leadership is seeing everyone in the image of God. I truly feel like every person matters in the environments I am responsible for. This is why inclusion is so important to me. Beyond seeing everyone as an individual to create an inclusive space, I recognize that each individual has inherent worth and value, and deserves to have a meaningful, safe experience.

Look carefully at your peer group. Are most of your friends like you in terms of . . .

- Religion?
- Citizenship?
- Race?
- Gender?
- Color?

- Socioeconomic class?
- Geographic proximity?
- Physical abilities?
- Sexual orientation?

Let's use that same lens with your leadership. Are the people on your team or in your group mostly like each other or not?

What recruiting and training can you do to make your social and leadership settings more diverse?

Inclusion doesn't take sides. As the comedian and disability advocate Pamela Rae Schuller says, "Inclusion is no longer about looking at people with special needs as a 'them.' It's about looking at our community as a 'we,' with every person having something to offer."

Inclusion doesn't create hierarchies based on ableism, race, ethnicity, popularity, money, or education. Inclusion means respectfully accounting for everyone's thoughts, feelings, and ideas, regardless of opinions or backgrounds. Here are some concrete ways to help you celebrate and cultivate inclusion wherever you find yourself in a leadership role:

- Try to create committees and board positions that include representation from everyone in your community.

- Invite speakers who can share their diverse stories and experiences.

- Make sure all programs you run accommodate and represent diversity.

- Find ways to share posts, texts, books, and articles by people from underrepresented backgrounds.

- Call out speech and actions that are extreme, offensive, or violent; that incite hate or make others feel excluded or condemned.

Celebrate the differences in your organization or group. The Torah describes the Jewish festivals as days of joy precisely because they are inclusive: "You, your sons and daughters, your male and female servants, the Levites in your towns, and the strangers, the fatherless and the widows living among you." (Deuteronomy 16:11) Some people mentioned in this list are family; some face difficult life circumstances. All are part of our extended community, showing us that when we're experiencing joy, it can be more meaningful when shared with others, even and especially with those who are not like us.

Jewish Bright Spot

The social activist Ruth Messinger has devoted her life to creating more just and diverse communities. She writes, "Part of being Jewish is to put Jewish values into practice where the poorest people are. This is not some new piece of Judaism: The rabbis and Jewish leaders have discussed the balance between helping Jews and non-Jews, the balance of working with different communities, the balance of showing who we are and building a better world not only for ourselves but for others."

1. What advice would you give people about finding the right balance Messinger mentions?

2. Many Jews live comfortably. What does Messinger mean when she says to put yourself "where the poorest people are"?

3. Giving too much can cause compassion fatigue—the kind of exhaustion that comes from doing too much for too many people and not caring for yourself. What strengthens you if you start to feel burned out from caring too much?

44

Getting Inspired and Staying Inspired

So what inspires you to lead? Some people are inspired to change the world because they see something broken that needs to be fixed. Others are inspired by watching role models and mentors. Some read biographies of remarkable people; some view documentaries and follow social media feeds of people they admire. Others find the commitment to keep going from meaningful quotes or stories.

For Gabriella, who we met in chapter 34, the Jewish value of creating a better future gives her the energy to continue: "My favorite aspect of everything that I do and my practice of Judaism is tikun olam. That's my driving force."

Inspiration is the force that motivates us to do something. It's the special holy feeling of being connected to something larger than ourselves. And it is powerful.

But inspiration waxes and wanes. To keep going, you've got to feel it again and again. Inspiration is not a one-shot deal.

Mettanna, nineteen, says Judaism inspired her to be more and do more: "I think there's a big difference between being a Jewish leader and a leader who happens to be Jewish. For a leader who happens to be Jewish, their identity doesn't affect how they do it. A Jewish leader uses Jewish wisdom and history with *kavanah* [intention] and is methodical about treating issues as Jewish problems." Write your own Jewish inspiration statement. You can begin like this:

● Judaism inspires me because . . .

Or

● The top three reasons I'm proud to be Jewish are . . .

Let's face it, you're not always going to feel inspired. Some days you're going to want to quit. We all have those moments. We asked teens to share what keeps them going when their inspiration hits a roadblock. Some are inspired, like Gabriella, by Jewish values: justice, kindness, and responsibility. Others look to Jewish heroes or specific biblical verses. Here are some of the responses we heard as we spoke to dozens of young leaders:

● "As Jews, we help each other out and lift each other up."

● "Something I love about Judaism is inclusivity, and growing Jewish leadership allows more people to be involved, to have a say in Judaism, and inspire others to have an enduring commitment to Jewish life and community."

- "I believe Judaism encourages us all to be leaders, so leadership is inherently Jewish."

- "Judaism teaches us to stand up for what is right and fight for what we believe in, no matter our age, which is the way I view leadership and something that has inspired me to become a leader in my community."

- "As Jews, we are taught to respect others. As a leader, you need to be able to accept new ideas and treat others respectfully in a group."

- "In order to be an effective leader, you must understand other people's opinions and feelings. By doing this, you can treat others how you would want to be treated by a leader, which is a strong Jewish value."

The sources of inspiration for young leaders are as varied as the teens themselves. For instance, Tali looks back on high school experiences that really inspired her:

> Some of the best leadership experiences I've had have had a Jewish text, charity, or social justice at the center—it makes leadership more of a godly task and offers a sense of mission.

Ezra told us he's inspired by *b'tzelem Elohim*, the idea that every single person is created "in the image of God," a term from the very first chapter of the Torah.

> The idea of being created in God's image allows me to recognize that all human beings can have amazing ideas no matter who they are, CEO or homeless—everyone has dreams and is worth hearing from.

Judah, seventeen, focuses on the Jewish heroes and role models he's studied in Bible and Talmud classes at his Jewish day school.

> I definitely draw on my Jewish education and experiences when leading. Judaism shapes a lot of my personality and almost all of my role models are Jewish—either living or textual role models, figures in the Torah and the Talmud and incorporated into my own life. When I'm leading, I sometimes have them in mind and think, "What would this person do in my position?"

High school tenth-grader Brooke has this to say about what inspires her Jewish leadership:

> As I've grown up in the Jewish community, I've seen that a lot of the qualities people look for in leadership are things I've found in my community. I think part of leadership is responding to people's needs; in the Jewish community, when people are in need, there are so many people willing to help you.

Amalia, who ran a large youth movement chapter in her neighborhood, said,

> I feel passionate about certain values: a love for Judaism, Torah, and Israel. When you feel connected, then you want to be involved and instill it in other people. To be a good leader, you need to be passionate about the values. If you don't care, then the people you're working with aren't going to care either.

Inner Workout

- As a society, we value values—but what exactly differentiates Jewish values from universal values?

- Can you think of a specific example of a time when Jewish values inspired you to help others?

- Which part of your Jewish identity would you like to emphasize more in your life?

Some leaders, like Shai, feel especially inspired by being an ambassador of their people:

> When I'm outside of Jewish circles, I feel it's important to be a good representative. Sometimes I'm the only Jew or in a minority, I think it's important to make an extra effort to be welcoming, not aggressive; inclusive, and not dominant. I go out of my way to be respectful, normal, cool, fun. That way I can bring a good name through my leadership.

Others said their passions and actions were ignited less by a particular Jewish value or teaching and more by their Jewish communities themselves:

- "If we didn't have so many institutions and opportunities in the Jewish community, I'm not sure I would have gotten involved."

- "I had a lot of opportunities in the Jewish community. There are things I started in seventh grade and am still doing now."

- "All of my leadership is for communities that raised me. . . . A lot of my leadership comes from the communities that helped develop me into me. It's kind of a way to give back."

Mia, nineteen, is a rabbi's daughter who knew a lot more about Judaism than many adults around her. She says,

> Everything is Jewish about my leadership. Everything we are taught is how to be a leader in this world. I wouldn't be half the person I am without my Jewish foundation. You open a Bible in your hotel room and you see Jewish leaders. We're learning from them. Judaism is a religion of leaders. We have literally all the tools. We've just got to pull them out and use them.

Whenever you experience a moment when you can't find the inspiration to keep leading, remember your values. Remind yourself of the best stories about people you've helped and the good work of the causes you support. Together, these can also help you create a unique leadership story that you can use to inspire others. We'll see how to tell that story in the next chapter.

Jewish Bright Spot

In the Torah, God asks us to live lives of holiness: "You shall not profane My holy name, that I may be sanctified in the midst of the Israelite people—I am Adonai who sanctifies you." (Leviticus 22:32) We do that through not acting in ways that would bring shame upon us, our families, or our people, and by seeking ways that elevate ourselves, our communities, and our relationship with God.

1. Describe the relationship among the three parts of this verse.

2. Give examples of the types of behavior that bring public shame on leaders.

3. List people who make you proud to be Jewish. Why?

45

Telling Your Jewish Leadership Story

Putting together everything you've learned about what motivates you in your leadership role—such as your values and your personal mission and vision statements we did together in part I—let's write your Jewish leadership story: a way of understanding and sharing why you lead. This will help you inspire others to join your cause, support your work, and raise awareness for issues you care about.

Why a story? The developmental psychologist and leadership expert Dr. Howard Gardner writes, "Stories constitute the single most powerful weapon in a leader's arsenal." Stories inspire us, stretch us, move us, and help fuel our imaginations. Leaders who can tell a meaningful story of their own growth and development—with all the highs and lows—can help their followers be brave, take risks, and then make bold steps toward creating future change.

Storytelling is a natural part of Jewish tradition; the Torah is filled with stories, as is the Talmud. Jewish continuity is, in part, about passing down stories and traditions. Many Holocaust survivors shared their eyewitness accounts and inspired us with their courage. World leaders, inventors, and opinion shapers write articles, essays, and memoirs to help us understand how they overcame challenges and imagined new realities.

Your Jewish leadership story gives you a chance to explain how you got involved with a cause and an organization, the meaning it gives your life, how your involvement has shaped your identity, and how it reflects your values, as you've discovered in some of the work you've done in this book so far.

As you think about all these parts of your story, you might want to begin by writing a timeline that includes major milestones in your life and leadership. Make sure to add significant Jewish events and developments. Great leadership stories often stress the hardships and struggles that people had to overcome (or have yet to overcome). When we see the difficulty of their journey from the inside, instead of simply the beautiful, polished, and edited exterior of success, their story resonates with us more deeply.

Inner Workout

As a leadership storyteller, ask yourself these questions as your story evolves over time:

- What Jewish events, places, rituals, or objects are meaningful to you and tell your story? You might even include a prop.
- Which Jewish individual inspires you?
- Is there a Jewish text or event in Jewish history that is particularly important to you? Why?
- Who inspires you as a leader?
- What leadership quotes inspire you?
- Do you have a mentor who encourages you? In what way?
- What is your main source of Jewish knowledge?
- What organization has most contributed to your leadership skills?
- What issues do you really care about or call you to action?
- Which Jewish values are most important to you?

Stories grab our attention when they include an engaging opening, a satisfying close, and specific and interesting details in the middle. Include what inspires you and the sights, smells, and tastes that make it come alive. Tell us about adversity in your life and how you overcame it, the cause you care about, your leadership goals, and how you have achieved (or intend to achieve) them.

As you begin telling your leadership story to others, you may want to think about the Jewish values, which we call "leadership superpowers," listed in the appendix and your relationship to them. Once you've outlined your story, tell it to others and incorporate their feedback.

Once you've written down and refined your leadership story, think about what you want to do with it. You might use it (the whole thing or just parts of it) when introducing yourself at an event. You might share it at a conference, convention, or meeting to talk about your organization's mission. You might pitch it to media outlets, such as local newspapers, to recruit new members, volunteers, or donors. You might use it in a job interview. You might post it. You might even use it with your parents, friends, or siblings to help them understand why you're investing so much of your time and energy in a cause you care about. Or simply read it every time you need to be inspired.

Israel's fourth prime minister, Golda Meir, once said, "Make the most of yourself by fanning the tiny, inner sparks of possibility into flames of achievement." When you create and share your Jewish leadership story, you take those inner sparks and start growing them into flames.

Jewish Bright Spot

The Passover seder revolves around storytelling, and the Torah is very clear that this is a key aspect of the holiday—and of Jewish life:

- "And when your children ask you . . ." (Exodus 12:26)

- "And you shall explain to your child on that day . . ." (Exodus 13:8)

- "And when, in time to come, your child asks you, saying, 'What does this mean?' you shall say . . ." (Exodus 13:14)

- "When in time your children ask you . . . you shall say . . ." (Deuteronomy 6:20–21)

1. What is different about these versions and why do we need more than one?

2. Why is storytelling from one generation to the next such a central Jewish responsibility?

3. Can you share a story that's been passed down in your family?

CLOSING THOUGHTS
BRINGING IT HOME

Thanks for reading *Dreaming Bigger*.

And an even bigger thanks for pushing forward on your Jewish leadership journey.

We know this book contains a lot of ideas and information, so here are ten questions to help you process what you've learned and integrate what you've read with your leadership experiences.

1. Looking at the table of contents, what chapter was most relevant to your leadership challenges? Why?

2. How about the opposite? What chapter was *least* relevant and why?

3. List the organizations or causes where you have a leadership role. Which one(s) would most benefit right now from your leadership expertise? Which might you drop?

4. Is there an adult—a professional or volunteer—you work with who you think would benefit from some of the leadership insights in this book?

5. Name something you've tried, experimented with, or incorporated into your leadership activities as a result of reading or discussing ideas in *Dreaming Bigger*.

6. Is there a teen mentioned in this book whose experience is close to your own?

7. Have you worked on your communication skills since you started this book? Describe what you're working on.

8. Have you thought about your own Jewish identity, relationship to Israel, or understanding of Jewish texts as a result of this leadership immersion?

9. Is there anything you read that you strongly agreed or disagreed with?

10. If you could add or write an additional chapter on teen leadership, what would it be?

As we wrote at the beginning, this book is part of a larger Jewish initiative to grow teen leaders. We believe in you, and we believe you can dream *even* bigger. Check out our animations, masterclasses, conversation cards, and more at DreamingBigger.org. Feel free to post your leadership story or your Jewish journey for other teens to read and share what resonated from this book. You can also ask questions or share your experiences so we can all grow from your wisdom.

Keep dreaming! Keep leading!

APPENDIX

Ten Leadership Superpowers

From our conversations with Jewish teens, professionals, and each other, we've distilled ten significant Jewish values—we call them "leadership superpowers."

1. **Jewish Peoplehood /** *Am Yisrael***:** In Judaism, prayer, charity, kindness, and study take place in community. Other people enhance the meaning and importance of our milestone and life-cycle events. This sense of belonging supports Jews through times of personal and national suffering and celebration. Some people take strength from feeling that Judaism gives them *mishpachah*—a large, extended family with each member of the family giving and receiving love. Do you feel a sense of belonging to this mishpachah? How can you strengthen it and make it as inclusive as possible?

2. **Torah Study /** *Limud HaTorah***:** Judaism has always placed a high value on knowledge and education for everyone, and Jewish life has been shaped by lifelong learning of sacred texts and their interpretation. Join this conversation across the ages with your own commentary. Do you know enough about Judaism to lead with confidence? How can you build on what you already know?

3. **Jewish Practice / Halachah:** One way to strengthen Jewish leadership is to identify core practices and behaviors that add meaning to your life. This could mean celebrating Shabbat and holidays that sanctify Jewish time, adding rituals that give structure to daily life, or taking on the practice of *chesed*—acts of loving-kindness. The word for Jewish law, *halachah*, comes from the Hebrew root "to go" or "to move," because Jewish practices help us move differently in the world. What's a Jewish practice that might add meaning to your life right now?

4. **Authenticity / *Aminut*:** The Hebrew word *aminut* also means "trustworthiness," "credibility," and "reliability." Our sages advise what they call *tocho k'voro*—ensuring that what's on the inside matches what's on the outside. The alignment of our inner and outer selves makes us truer to who we are. We are each uniquely created; there is no one else like you, so it's best to be yourself. Sophia Zalik, a teen leader from Atlanta, has written a powerful poem reminding us to surround ourselves with people who respect and love us for who we really are. She reminds us that real friends want us to be fully ourselves.

Sometimes you feel like the world's gonna blow
The self-conscious finally starts to show
How will you ever know
Your world might be going slow
Is it in my head
When I'm laying in bed
Is it something I did
I'm sorry I'm just a kid
Don't be so 2-faced
Just tell me in the first place
You build me up to take me down
So you're just a fake friend
Did I get too attached
There so easy to take
One day there one day gone

— Sophia Zalik

5. **Honesty / *Emet*:** Truth-telling isn't always easy, especially when we must own our mistakes and use language accurately to create genuine credibility. Authenticity is being true to yourself. Honesty is being true with others. These are characteristics people expect from their leaders. Anything less can harm trust. This means using language responsibly, minimizing toxic talk, and handling money and messaging with accuracy.

6. **Integrity / *Yashrut*:** Integrity in Hebrew comes from *yashar*, the root for "straight." As we read in Proverbs (2:20): "Follow the way of the good and keep to the paths of the just." Integrity demands that we are consistent in our actions, straight with others, and call out bad behaviors. As a leader, you're entrusted with all kinds of private information, and you need to keep it private. When someone confides in us, they expect us to honor their trust just as we want others to respect our privacy.

7. **Responsibility / *Achrayut*:** Being responsible means responding when something is broken, stepping in to fix it, and following through until the job gets done. Teen leaders who are responsible are accountable and reliable. Ezra, the great scribe and leader who transformed the ancient Jewish community that had returned from exile to the Land of Israel millennia ago, captures this sentiment when he said "Take action, for the responsibility is yours and we are with you. Act with resolve!" (Ezra 10:4)

8. **Kindness / *Chesed*:** The Bible tells us that "the world is built on loving-kindness." (Psalm 89.3) Being considerate, friendly, and generous with our time and compliments are all expressions of compassion. Having compassionate eyes allows us to see the needs of others—their loneliness, their struggles, their situation—and we are able to respond with acts of kindness. In the Talmud, God is referred to as "The Compassionate One." Maimonides, the famous twelfth-century Jewish philosopher and physician, wrote that all the actions that demonstrate kindness—visiting the sick, helping a bride, burying the dead—"are all physical acts of kindness, and there are no limits to what one must do to fill these requirements."

9. **Discipline / *Mishma'at*:** The Hebrew word *mishma'at* comes from the root meaning "listen." (The same root is at the heart of the word *shema*.) There is a relationship between listening and being disciplined. It implies hearing your own voice of wisdom and that of others. The impulse to

do good in the world as a leader has to be balanced with the discipline to stick to projects and plans until they're done. Rabbi Abraham Joshua Heschel put it well: "Self-respect is the fruit of discipline; the sense of dignity grows with the ability to say no to oneself." When you can discipline yourself to reach your goals, you enhance your self-respect.

10. **Humility / *Anavah*:** A healthy ego is central to good leadership—and so is modesty. Moses, who brought the Jews out of slavery and to the Promised Land, was also called the world's most humble human in the book of Numbers (12:3). Jim Collins, in his bestselling book on leadership *Good to Great*, writes, "The difference between a good leader and a great leader is humility." Great leaders have a lot of ambition, but it's not for themselves; it's for others and for causes they care about. We can't accomplish anything in leadership by ourselves. It's always about the team.

Inner Workout

Use this space to articulate your personal leadership superpowers. Pick three or five or seven. Whatever number works for you. Feel free to borrow from the list above or choose your own.

1.

2.

3.

4.

5.

6.

7.

A Note from the Authors

Dear Friends,

Thanks for traveling together with us on this incredible journey. We wanted to say goodbye with a few words about ourselves. We come from two different hemispheres but share one love: the Jewish people. We've both devoted our personal and professional lives to serving the Jewish community. We were each teen leaders, and we've encountered thousands of teen leaders.

When we were teens, we learned to organize, recruit, speak publicly, raise money, manage our time, and raise awareness of important issues. These skills have served us in every facet of our personal and professional adult lives. We also made loads of mistakes, and those mistakes were some of our most important teachers.

As we each got more involved in leadership development, we saw that many of the people who have roles today as volunteers and professionals—from CEOs to educators, from heads of camps to heads of foundations, from leaders of movements to leaders of organizations—followed a similar path to ours. They got involved as teens in youth movements, in clubs, or on sports teams.

Many teens take on leadership roles without official titles, so they don't always get the recognition they deserve. There are also many who find fulfillment in following rather than leading and that, too, is an amazing contribution. When we use the word *leader* in this book, we mean anyone who wants to work on behalf of others and causes they care about. Almost everyone leads in some area or at some time in their lives—in their families, among friends, or in their communities. We can't wait to hear about your Jewish leadership story.

With blessings for the leadership journey,

Erica and Benji

ACKNOWLEDGMENTS

To all the teens who contributed to this book by sharing your challenges, your talents, and your guidance: You are powerful. You have influence. You can make things better. Discover your gifts because our world needs your talent to reform politics, the environment, poverty, hunger . . . and the list goes on.

We'd also like to thank the remarkable people who supported the publication of this book as part of our larger teen initiative: David Behrman, Dena Neusner, Tzivia MacLeod, Emily Wichland, and the whole Behrman House team for their support and excellent stewardship of this book.

A huge shout-out to all the professionals and volunteers we interviewed, who shared thoughts and insights and who commented on earlier drafts. In particular: Michelle Shapiro Abraham, Rabbi David Bashevkin, Rabbi Scot A. Berman, Matti Borowski, Dr. David Bryfman, Adam Cohen, Talia Diamond, Becky Dunkel, Rafi Engelhart, Gideon Fine, Wayne Green, Rabbi Micah Greenland, Matthew Grossman, Elisheva Hadad, Talia Kliot, Keren Lax, Benjamin Lee, Haylee Mevorah, Avi Orlow, Romi Rubanovich, Penina Shtauber, Adam Smith, Jodi Sperling, Shuki Taylor, Jessica Vinokur, Gila Weiner, and Talya Wiseman. Thank you for being incredible partners, mentors, and friends and investing your talent into our emerging leaders. You are growers.

We'd also like to thank the incredible funders who made this happen. We deeply appreciate the encouragement and support of the Zalik Family Foundation, who catalyzed this work. In addition, we thank Gary and Carol Berman, Martine and Stanley Fleishman, the Goodman Foundation, JNF Australia, the Leven Foundation, and the Maimonides Fund. We thank our friends at the Mayberg Foundation for bringing us together, and the Mayberg Center, Keshev, and Israel Impact Partners for providing a professional home as we brought this to life.

We also want to acknowledge the researchers and practitioners, in addition to those whom we mentioned above, who have spent a lot of time and thought investigating the formative stage that is adolescence and have given us the fruit of their prodigious labors either in conversation or writing or both: Arielle Levites, Liat Sayfan, Alex Pomson, Frayda Gonshor Cohen, Pearl Mattenson, Zohar Rotem, and Katherine Schwartz. We also want to thank several organizations that have supported Jewish teen research: the Jewish Education Project, the Jim Joseph Foundation, the Jewish Teen Education and Engagement Funder Collaborative, Lippman Kanfer Foundation for Living Torah, and Rosov Consulting. By making Jewish teens an important subject of study, you have elevated the attention to this emerging generation of sacred leaders and followers. Thank you.

But most of all, we want to thank the many teens we spoke to who humanized and personalized the ideas in this book and these specific teens who participated in lengthy interviews: Abby, Alex, Amalia, Ari, Audrey, Avi, Ben, Brooke, Eyden, Ezra, Gabriella, Gavi times two, Hannah, Ilan, Jon, Judah, Josh times four, Mia, Penina, Racheli, Rami, Romi, Sam, Sara, Shai, Shira, Tali, Yakova, and Zachary times two. At times, because they asked, we changed their names and identifying information to protect their privacy. We are grateful that you made the time to respond to surveys, share your ideas, give comments on chapters, and meet with us. We appreciate the fact that you spoke up and shared your voices, passions, and frustrations. You represent the core of this book and this initiative. We are moved by your stories, commitments, and sense of urgency and can't wait to see the way each of you will rock our world.

Finally, thank *you!* Thank you for reading this book, for reflecting, for engaging with us, and for bringing the unique voice that only you can bring to the world. It is a voice we need and truly value!

BIBLIOGRAPHY

Bennis, Warren G. *On Becoming a Leader*. New York: Basic Books, 2009.

Buchdahl, Angela Warnick. "My Personal Story: Kimchee on the Seder Plate." *Sh'ma: A Journal of Jewish Responsibility* (June 2003), https://18doors.org/my_personal _story_kimchee_on_the_seder_plate/.

Cain, Susan. *Quiet: The Power of Introverts in a World That Can't Stop Talking*. New York: Broadway Paperbacks, 2013.

Collins, Jim. *Good to Great: Why Some Companies Make the Leap and Others Don't*. New York: HarperBusiness, 2001.

Daniels, Jordan. "Creating Belonging for Jews of Color." *EJewishPhilanthropy* (2019), https://ejewishphilanthropy.com/creating-belonging-for-jews-of-color/.

Heumann, Judy. *Being Heumann: An Unrepentant Memoir of a Disability Rights Activist*. Boston: Beacon Press, 2020.

Jones, Laurie Beth. *The Path: Creating Your Mission Statement for Work and for Life*. New York: Hachette, 2001.

Kaplan, Mordecai M. *Judaism as a Civilization: Toward a Reconstruction of American-Jewish Life*. Philadelphia: Jewish Publication Society, 2010.

Lapin, David. *Lead by Greatness: How Character Can Power Your Success*. Avoda Books, 2012.

Levites, Arielle, and Liat Sayfan. "Gen Z Now: Understanding and Connecting with Today's Jewish Teens." Jewish Education Project and Rosov Consulting, https:// www.rosovconsulting.com/wp-content/uploads/2019/03/JEP_GenZ_report _revised_5.14.19_composite.pdf.

Levy, Daniella. *By Light of Hidden Candles*. St. Paul, MN: Kasva Press, 2007.

Lipstadt, Deborah E. *Antisemitism: Here and Now*. New York: Schocken, 2019.

Messinger, Ruth. "Ruth Messinger: We Must Help, and in the Right Ways." Interview by Amy Klein. Jewish Telegraphic Agency, August 24, 2009, https://www.jta.org /2009/08/24/lifestyle/ruth-messinger-we-must-help-and-in-the-right-ways.

Pliskin, Zelig, *Gateway to Self-Knowledge*. Jerusalem: Aish HaTorah, 1986.

Rath, Tom. *StrengthsFinder 2.0*. New York: Simon and Schuster, 2007.

Rubinfeld, Kendra. "Jewish Mentor of the Month: Antiracist Powerhouse, Deitra Reiser." GatherDC, February 15, 2021, https://gatherdc.org/2021/02/15/jewish-mentor-of -the-month-antiracist-powerhouse-deitra-reiser/.

Sacks, Jonathan. "Three Approaches to Dreams." Jonathan Sacks: The Rabbi Sacks Legacy Trust, 2013, https://www.rabbisacks.org/covenant-conversation/mikketz/three -approaches-to-dreams/.

Schuller, Pamela Rae. "The Two Little Words That Can Change a Life," ELI Talks, August 4, 2015, YouTube video, 13:18. https://www.youtube.com/watch?v=COJvIrVoD-4.

Schwartz, Barry. *The Paradox of Choice: Why More Is Less*. New York: Ecco, 2004.

Tatz, Akiva. *The Thinking Jewish Teenager's Guide to Life*. Southfield, MI: Targum Press, 1999.

Telushkin, Joseph. *Words That Help, Words That Heal*. New York: William Morrow, 2019.

Weiss, Bari. *How to Fight Anti-Semitism*. New York: Crown, 2019.

Yousafzai, Malala. *I Am Malala: The Girl Who Stood Up For Education and Was Shot by the Taliban*. New York: Little, Brown, 2013.

About the Authors

Dr. Erica Brown

Dr. Erica Brown is the vice provost for values and leadership at Yeshiva University and the founding director of its Rabbi Lord Jonathan Sacks-Herenstein Center for Values and Leadership. She previously served as the director of the Mayberg Center for Jewish Education and Leadership and as an associate professor of curriculum and pedagogy at the George Washington University. Erica is the author of twelve books on leadership, the Hebrew Bible, and spirituality. Her latest book, *Esther: Power, Fate and Fragility in Exile* (Maggid), was a finalist for the National Jewish Book Award. Her book *Ecclesiastes and the Search for Meaning* is forthcoming from Maggid. Erica has a daily podcast, "Take Your Soul to Work."

Erica is also the author of *Jonah: The Reluctant Prophet* (Maggid), *Take Your Soul to Work: 365 Meditations on Every Day Leadership* (Simon and Schuster), and *Happier Endings: A Meditation on Life and Death* (Simon and Schuster), which won the Wilbur Award and Nautilus Award for spiritual writing. Her previous books include *Inspired Jewish Leadership*, which was a National Jewish Book Award finalist; *Spiritual Boredom*, and *Confronting Scandal* (all from Jewish Lights). She coauthored *The Case for Jewish Peoplehood* (Jewish Lights). She also wrote *Seder Talk: A Conversational Haggada*, *Leadership in the Wilderness*, *In the Narrow Places*, and *Return: Daily Inspiration for the Days of Awe* (all from OU/Koren). She is currently working on a commentary on Ecclesiastes (Maggid).

She has been published in the *New York Times*, *The Atlantic*, *Tablet*, *First Things*, and *The Jewish Review of Books*, and she wrote a monthly column for the *New York Jewish Week* for several years. She has blogged for *Psychology Today*, *Newsweek/Washington Post's* "On Faith," and JTA, and tweeted on one page of Talmud study a day at @DrEricaBrown for the seven-and-a-half-year cycle. She has master's degrees from the Institute of Education (University of London), Jews' College (University of London), and

Harvard University, and a PhD from Baltimore Hebrew University. Erica was a Jerusalem Fellow, is a faculty member of the Wexner Foundation, an Avi Chai Fellow, and the recipient of the 2009 Covenant Award for her work in education. She was the scholar-in-residence at the Jewish Federation of Greater Washington and the Combined Jewish Philanthropies of Boston, and the community scholar for the Jewish Center of New York. She currently serves as a community scholar for Congregation Etz Chaim in Livingston, New Jersey.

Rabbi Dr. Benji Levy

Rabbi Dr. Benji Levy is a founder of Israel Impact Partners, which works with funders to accelerate the growth of the nonprofits they care about, bringing together consultants, implementation specialists, and functional experts to effect transformational change. He is also a founder of Keshev, providing mental health support, therapy, and education.

Rabbi Benji served as CEO of Mosaic United, a historic joint venture partnership between Israel and global Jewry to strengthen Jewish identity and connections to Israel for youth around the world. Previously he served as the dean of Moriah College in Sydney, Australia, one of the largest Jewish schools in the world.

Rabbi Benji was named as one of three top global changemakers working for Diaspora Jewry by the Israeli newspaper *Makor Rishon*, and awarded Educator of the Year by JNF for his service to the Australian Jewish community. He received an Australian Postgraduate Award for his research in Jewish identity; published *Covenant and the Jewish Conversion Question: Extending the Thought of Rabbi Joseph B. Soloveitchik* (Palgrave Macmillan) and *An Oasis In Time: Seven Thoughts for the Seventh Day* (Maggid), and shares many ideas through multiple mediums including www.RabbiBenji.com and @RabbiBenji. He serves as a reservist in the Spokesperson Unit of the Israel Defense Forces.

Rabbi Benji has a doctorate in philosophy from the University of Sydney and received rabbinic ordination following his study at Yeshivat Har Etzion. He was awarded first-class honors in Jewish civilization thought and culture; he has a BA in media and communications from the University of Sydney and an education degree from Herzog College, and he completed the Lookstein Center Principals' Program at Bar-Ilan University.

Jewish Youth Pledge

A pledge is an oath, a promise, or a commitment. It's a way that we affirm our values and hold ourselves accountable to them. The Jewish Youth Pledge invites Jewish teens and young adults around the globe to commit to being active, contributing members of the Jewish community throughout their lives. The Pledge aims to ignite a surge in Jewish pride that will equip Jewish youth with the confidence to contribute to a strong Jewish future through their action.

I, _____ hereby pledge ...
(name)

to act today and throughout my lifetime to strengthen the Jewish people and Israel.

I make this commitment _____
(date)

because I have a responsibility to ensure that my generation writes the next

chapter of the Jewish story and remains a strong link in the chain of generations.

Jewish
Youth
PLEDGE

_____   _____
DATE   FOR GENERATIONS TO COME   SIGNATURE

CPSIA information can be obtained
at www.ICGtesting.com
Printed in the USA
JSHW012110120922
30435JS00002B/2